D1604408

I. *Ad Drop Sketch,* cat. 12

II. Eugene Gilboe, *Ad Drop Sketch, c.*
1929, cat. 45

III. *Olio Drop Sketch*, cat. 56

IV. John Z. Wood, *Drop Curtain Sketch of "At the Fountain—Spain,"* cat. 4

POPULAR ENTERTAINMENT   1895-1929

THE Twin City Scenic COLLECTION

April 5—June 14, 1987

University Art Museum
University of Minnesota
Minneapolis

Front cover: *Drop Curtain Sketch*, (cat. 6), c. 1923, water-color on paper
    Collection of the Performing Arts Archives,
    University of Minnesota Libraries
Back cover: Pencil inscription on reverse of *Drop Curtain Sketch* illustrated on front cover; John Z. Wood, *Drop Curtain Sketch of Venice*, (cat. 7), c. 1923, watercolor on paper, Collection of the Performing Arts Archives, University of Minnesota Libraries; Twin City Scenic stationery logo, 1920s, Collection of the Performing Arts Archives, University of Minnesota Libraries

Design: Evans-Smith & Skubic Incorporated
Photo Credits: Tim Rummelhoff

This exhibition was supported in part by grants from the National Endowment for the Humanities (NEH), a federal agency, Washington, D.C., and the National Conference of the United States Institute for Theatre Technology (USITT). Further support of the project was provided by the Minnesota Humanities Commission in cooperation with the National Endowment for the Humanities and the Minnesota State Legislature. A portion of the University Art Museum's operating funds for this fiscal year has been provided through a grant from the Institute of Museum Services (IMS), a federal agency that offers support to the nation's museums.

Contents

Note to the Reader

In accordance with the practice of theatre professionals, this catalogue uses two different spellings for the word "theater." "Theatre" should be understood to mean the legimate and popular priced theatre, including vaudeville, whereas "theater" indicates motion picture houses and the saloon and variety halls which presented a less refined type of entertainment.

Twin City Scenic was originally called the Twin City Scenic Studio. It later was more often known as the Twin City Scenic Company, but either name continued to appear on the scenery it produced. The two names were used almost interchangeably, and the authors of the essays in this catalogue have followed that practice.

In Dedication

The late nineteenth and early twentieth centuries in America are rich in theatrical history, but little remains of the romantic tradition of painted scenery. As each year passes, there are fewer who can recall the beauty and delight evoked by a finely executed painted drop. For the very nature of scenery implies its fugitive quality. One interesting aspect of this painterly tradition, the ad curtain, is nearly gone and forgotten, for even those who remember seeing them in the theatres have their memories dimmed. Theatrical history today tends to look upon turn-of-the-century scenery through the eyes of the reformers of the "New Stagecraft" such as Hiram Moderwell: "We now rarely see an old-fashioned 'drop' scene, and have almost forgotten how absurd it looks." [H. Moderwell, *Theatre of Today* (New York: John Lane Company, 1914), 21.] Today the ad curtain is occasionally used in revivals of melodramas so that the audience can hiss at the villain, smile at the scenery, and feel self-satisfied with the sophistication of the 1980s.

The theatre of 1880, however, was vital almost beyond our imagination, consisting of perhaps 2,000 working theatres across the country with an audience made up of nearly every citizen. As a part of the scenic tradition of this period, the phenomenon of the ad curtain interestingly illustrates the commercial course of our cultural evolution.

John R. Rothgeb

These two paragraphs were found with John Rothgeb's unfinished essay, which is included in this catalogue. The contents of the paragraphs are the embodiment of John Rothgeb's feelings and understanding of an era of the theatre where scenic spectacle and splendor fulfilled the audience's every expectation. Although John had a real commitment to the principles of the "New Stagecraft" that have so strongly shaped scenic design in the twentieth century, he had a passion for the late nineteenth century and for all of the marvels and wonderment that visually dominated theatre. Because the scenic remnants of this period have been either lost or, for the most part, destroyed, John felt that today's public has a bias against late Victorian theatre, resulting from too few artifacts from which to judge the beauty and splendor of the late nineteenth-century stage.

It is unfortunate that John Rothgeb's untimely death on December 3, 1986 prevented him from completing his contribution to the *Twin City Scenic* exhibition. He had been an active part of this project from the very beginning, providing advice on the collection, consulting on the scope and direction of the exhibit, and giving the necessary historical perspective of the times and processes that he had so much at his command. His contagious enthusiasm for this project has been a real force in shaping the initial thinking on the historical importance and significance of the materials in this exhibit, and he offered tremendous assistance on how best to convey that information to the public.

This catalogue is dedicated to John R. Rothgeb and to the contributions he made to the research and documentation of the tradition of scenic art that was the moving force of late nineteenth-century theatre. He will be missed, but the groundwork that he established will provide the necessary foundation ultimately to preserve for future generations both an integral link with the nineteenth-century heritage of American theatre and an understanding of "the romantic tradition of painted scenery."

Foreword

This exhibition began with a phone call from Lance Brockman, an associate professor in the Theatre Arts Department at the University, telling me that the USITT (United States Institute for Theatre Technology) would be meeting in the Twin Cities in a couple of years. He asked me if the Museum would be willing to put up a small exhibit of material made by a company called Twin City Scenic. The Museum is always open to ideas for interesting exhibitions, and so I made an appointment to visit the Performing Arts Archives where the Twin City Scenic materials were stored. I was immediately entranced with what I saw and convinced that it would make a wonderful exhibition.

Lance showed me hundreds of drawings, watercolors, and gouaches. I'm sure I saw the design for the curtain I remembered from my grade school auditorium stage, but with blank compartments where the local advertising had been. I saw garden scenes, street scenes, and fanciful room settings. I saw exotic, eastern environments with camels, dragons, and bejeweled cave interiors. I was particularly taken with a miniature stage that featured a toy automobile and a moving road, curtains that opened and closed, and lights that flashed different colors.

I was impressed, too, with Lance's depth of knowledge about the Twin City Scenic Company and his breadth of knowledge about the history of scenic design, in general. The happy combination of resources that make good exhibitions—an interesting collection accompanied by a person with specialized expertise—had just dropped into our laps! We began to plan the exhibition immediately.

It was fortunate that Lance called when he did. Because we had some lead time, we were able to work with him to secure a major grant from the National Endowment for the Humanities. We also received financial assistance from the USITT and the Minnesota Humanities Commission. With this we have put together

1. *Drop Curtain Sketch*, cat. 3

opposite:
2. Line drawing by Arthur Hurtt showing the backstage of the Bijou Opera House with its various line sets to raise and lower the scenery. Arthur Hurtt was a scenic artist for Twin City Scenic Company from 1896 to 1909. (Photo: Courtesy of the Theodore L. Hays Papers, Minnesota Historical Society)

an exhibition, catalogue, and several public programs. Some feature the Twin City Scenic Company in the context of popular entertainment from America at the turn of the century until the movies crowded vaudeville out of the public mind. Others provide a comparison between theatre design then and now.

A second exhibition called *Contemporary Theatre Set Design in the Twin Cities* was intended to be an ancillary exhibition but has taken on a life of its own. This exhibit, not included in this catalogue, represents the most important contemporary theatre set designs from several of the more than 100 Twin Cities theatres. A brief exhibition of extant, full-scale theatre drops made by the Twin City Scenic Company and a symposium will round out the University's activities.

The Twin City Scenic Company existed from about 1895 until 1979, though after the late 1920s it stopped producing the lavish illusionistic backdrops shown here. It moved several times in its long existence and had branches all over the country. In the heyday of the Studio, around the turn of the century and up until the late 1920s, salesmen toured the country taking along these beautifully painted 'miniatures' of the full-scale scenic possibilities. When a theatre made an order, the salesman phoned or telegraphed it in, and an amazingly short time later the sets were completely painted and ready to be shipped on the next train out.

Unfortunately the records that would have led to possible sources of full-scale sets made by the Twin City Scenic Company were destroyed. Lance has been able to find several, however, and is constantly on the lookout for more. The materials in this exhibition were saved from a 1980 fire and were tracked down by Lance through former Twin City Scenic employees. The collection was ultimately donated to the University by W. R. Brown, a past president, in 1984. The Twin City Scenic archival collection, now a part of the University of Minnesota Libraries, of which the materials on exhibit are a part, include about 1,500 paintings and drawings (primarily watercolors and gouaches), about 500 photographs, and several models used to demonstrate various kinds of stage equipment. It is the most complete archive of a single scenic company anywhere in the United States over such a long period of time.

While this archive concentrates on only one company, the completeness of the archive allows documentation of the changes in the entire stage scene industry in the United States, and through that, changes in the theatre itself. A study of the Twin City Scenic Collection reveals stylistic changes in scenic design—some because of the influence of style changes in 'high art' and some because of the changes in the role of the theatre in everyday life. The University is indeed fortunate that Lance Brockman's sleuthing, with the generosity of W.R. Brown, has made it a unique resource for the study of the history of the theatre.

I am grateful to Lance Brockman for giving us the opportunity to exhibit the Twin City Scenic material and also for the opportunity to work with him. He served as special curator for all three of the exhibitions—*Twin City Scenic*, *Contemporary Theatre Set Designs*, and *Extant Stage Scenery*. I can say without hesitation that Lance is the most well-organized curator that we have ever worked with who had had no previous museum experience, and better organized than many who had worked with museums numerous times. It has been a real pleasure to work with someone so well versed in his subject, so well organized, and so open to accepting our suggestions about display and publication.

Lance's assistant Eric Hagen was also helpful with many details, and Rick Polenek served as a special consultant on the exhibition of contemporary theatre set designs. We are also grateful for the cooperation of Alan Lathrop, curator of the Performing Arts Archives at the University.

The Museum staff put out extra special effort to make this exhibition educational and at the same time provide the proper theatrical ambiance to set off the works. Susan Brown, associate director, oversaw the publication of the catalogue and other printed materials under especially harrowing circumstances. William Lampe, our technical director whose background is in the theatre, worked with Lance and Eric on the installation design, as did Ian Dudley, Museum preparator. John Sonderegger, Steven Williams, and Michael Bailey did a masterful

job of framing all of the somewhat fragile watercolors, gouaches, and drawings in a manner that was attractive and gave a period flavor, yet was sound in terms of conservation. Karen Lovaas, registrar, and her assistant, Cindy Collins, organized the materials wonderfully, as usual, and Lisa Hartwig, public relations and special events coordinator made our theatre special events truly theatrical. Fiona Irving, our new curator, stepped right in and helped with the exhibition of contemporary theatre designs. Melanie Marshall, acting principal secretary, performed all sorts of tasks with her usual good humor and efficient style, as did her assistant, Gwen Sutter, and pinch hitters, acting editor Kathryn Hong and museum assistant Jane Healey. Cori Kulzer, accounts supervisor, supervised the accounts to keep us in the black all the time. Wearing her sales shop manager hat, she also arranged for the production of slide sets and other special sales items. We appreciate the assistance of Kent Neely, managing director of the University's Rarig Theatre, in publicizing the project. We wish also to thank Carol Evans-Smith and Ned Skubic, whose fine creative talents were applied lavishly to this catalogue and all the printed materials for this project.

Thanks also to Robert Moulton and his students from the Theatre Arts and Music Departments, who presented a performance of "songs, dance, and snappy patter" entitled *Backstage at the Bijou* (named for one of the early homes of the Twin City Scenic Company—the backstage of the old Bijou Opera House on Washington Avenue) to open this exhibition. From the volunteer Advisory Board of the Colleagues of the University Art Museum, Jane Thompson chaired our opening committee, and we owe her a special vote of thanks, as we do all our volunteers who help make our programs successful.

Lyndel King
Director

Curator's Acknowledgments

It is a difficult task to recount all those who have shared their time and talents in preparing this exhibit. It is one, however, undertaken with pleasure and much gratitude to everyone who has helped shape this project. First and foremost, we are all indebted to William Robert Brown, who donated the Twin City Scenic Collection to the Performing Arts Archives of the University of Minnesota. Mr. Brown has also generously shared his time and information which was invaluable in reconstructing the history of one of the most successful scenic studios in this country after the turn of the century. His family's involvement in the company dates back to the 1890s and, through his grandfather, William Knox Brown, and his father, Calvin Robert Brown, there is an established lineage that makes an understanding of both the scenic demands and the artifacts of this lost era available to us today.

Thanks to Alan Lathrop, curator, for providing a home for the collection at the Performing Arts Archives. Alan has shared his expertise in archival documentation and preservation, enabling us to clean, index, and prepare the Twin City Scenic Collection for interpretation and use by both students and scholars. I also owe a special debt of gratitude to my graduate research assistants, Pam Kildahl and Eric Hagen, who spent many long hours tracking down obscure information in various libraries, including that of the Minnesota Historical Society, and assisting in the location of extant scenery in this region. Their services through the initial research and implementation of this project were made possible through a Grant-in-Aid from the Graduate School of the University.

No exhibit takes place without the dedication and commitment of museum personnel and staff. This monumental undertaking was facilitated by the extremely helpful and cooperative staff of the University Art Museum, which has my unqualified praise and appreciation. I am forever grateful to its director Lyndel

3. John Z. Wood, *Drop Curtain Sketch of "Belangona Castle — Switzerland,"* cat. 5

King for originally seeing the potential of the materials in the collection, for helping me through the funding process, and for providing the leadership required to realize my ideas and dreams. Lyndel acted as the catalyst throughout the whole process, helping to shape my thoughts and to move the project forward. Without her expertise and assistance this exhibit would never have reached its full potential.

Thanks are also due to the Museum staff who have worked directly with the exhibit, the catalogue, and the didactic panels necessary to explain the variety of visual materials: to John Jenswold, former Museum editor, for his help in securing the services of graphic designers Carol Evans-Smith and Ned Skubic to coordinate the visual look of the project; to Susan Brown, associate director, who edited the catalogue and to Kathryn Hong, acting editor, who edited the exhibition text panels; to Bill Lampe, technical director, for his help in devising and implementing the installation of the exhibit; to Ian Dudley and John Sonderegger, preparators, who assisted with the installations; to Karen Lovaas, registrar, for her ability to organize and juggle all of the administrative details and facilitate the transfer of the materials for exhibit; to Lisa Hartwig and Kent Neely for their invaluable assistance in publicizing the exhibit.

I want to extend special thanks to Forrest Newlin, theatre designer at Texas Tech University, for his encouragement and for revealing to me, as a student, the fun and excitement of scenic design. In addition, I am grateful for his willingness to provide comments for this catalogue on short notice when another author was unable, for personal reasons, to complete his obligation.

The cooperation and encouragement of my colleagues in the Department of Theatre Arts has been a tremendous asset. I am especially indebted to Jean Montgomery who provided necessary proofreading of copy for my grant proposals and catalogue entries. She has also assisted me by undertaking several of my production responsibilities during the mounting of this exhibit. Kent Neely has acted as a sounding board for many of my early ideas about how I could utilize the resources of the Twin City Scenic Collection. To the faculty of the Department of

4. *Conservatory Drop Sketch*, cat. 13

Theatre Arts I would like to express my appreciation.

Contemporary Theatre Set Design in the Twin Cities, the exhibit which accompanies that of the Twin City Scenic Collection, is a valuable tool for interpreting current trends in scenic design as well as for analyzing the effects of our heritage. I am indebted to the various designers and theatres in the Twin Cities that have generously given of their time, enthusiasm, and resources for this project. Rick Polenek has shared his expertise on exhibit design and has expended a tremendous amount of time and commitment to coordinating the installation of the design pieces for this supporting exhibit.

Perhaps the largest debt of gratitude goes to the National Endowment for the Humanities whose sizable grant in large part financed the exhibitions and publications. NEH support of this project came at a critical time when the resources of the collection were relatively unknown, and, yet, the Endowment was willing to back this undertaking, thereby making a unique interpretation of popular entertainment available to the public. In addition, the United States Institute for Theatre Technology not only provided monetary support for this project but was willing to feature the collection and to devote sessions to an interpretation of the materials at its national conference held in Minneapolis, April 21 to 25, 1987.

The evaluation and analysis of the extensive resources of the Twin City Scenic Collection are ongoing processes and the ultimate value of the collection, for both historical research and practical application of the materials, is left to future interpretation. It is hoped that this exhibit will begin to illuminate that critical period when the theatre had precipitously arrived at the crossroads of the twentieth century with the uncanny premonition that the motion picture camera was destined to dethrone theatre as the king of popular entertainment.

C. Lance Brockman

5. *Garden Drop Sketch*, cat. 15

16

Theatre Space as Social Space:
The Twin City Scenic Collection

George Lipsitz

George Lipsitz is a cultural historian and assistant professor of American Studies at the University of Minnesota, Minneapolis.

The sketches, watercolor renderings, and models on display in *The Twin City Scenic Collection* offer contemporary viewers a rare glimpse at the styles and conventions of visual representation prevalent in American theatres between 1895 and 1929. During those years, the images and icons of set design responded to changing aesthetic tastes as well as to evolving commercial imperatives. Each dramatic genre and each form of theatrical production encouraged a corresponding style of visual representation. Thus the evolution of popular theatre—from melodrama to vaudeville to motion pictures—found concomitant expression in a continuum of romantic, realist, and modern images.

Yet theatre space is not just aesthetic space. It is also a place for experiments with new beliefs and behavior made possible or necessary by changes in society. When Americans went to the theatre between 1895 and 1929, they experienced fundamentally new uses of theatrical spaces and performances. In previous years, churches, lodge halls, and community centers served as places for theatrical productions designed to mark festive occasions like weddings and holidays. Commercial theatres needed no special occasions and no connections to other activities to justify their plays, musicals, and skits. Instead, they carved away a new

opposite:
6. *Ad Drop Sketch*, cat. 12

kind of social space—buildings devoted exclusively to use for leisure activities. In addition, theatrical performances became commodities sold to strangers for an agreed upon price, rather than collective creations by communities enacting rituals to maintain solidarity and group identity. The social act of going to the theatre as well as the content of theatrical productions in those years reflected and shaped fundamentally new attitudes about art, leisure, and community.

Theatre as a Social Problem in Minneapolis and St. Paul

Throughout the nineteenth century, religious, cultural, and educational authorities in the Twin Cities worried about the dangers posed to community values by the commercial theatre. In 1857, Reverend Charles Seccombe of the First Congregational Church in St. Anthony preached a sermon advising young men to avoid the evils of theatrical performances. Seccombe claimed that theatre "does violence to the moral feelings and virtue of the audience," and he complained that "nothing is more common than indecent expressions and allusions in the plays there presented." The pastor continued his critique by noting that "the men and women who appear on the stage are usually persons of bad character, and the tendency upon the audience is to render it likewise." Seccombe concluded that the evils of theatre emanated from its basic mission rather than from abuses of it, arguing that "the very features that most shock a correct moral sense are assigned a prominent place."[1]

Reverend Seccombe's attack upon the theatre may strike modern readers as hopelessly old-fashioned and unduly alarmist, but his hyperbole should alert us to the seriousness of the issues involved in evaluating the social meaning of theatrical presentations. Our inability to comprehend the urgency of Seccombe's diatribe may stem less from our sophistication and refinement than from the ways in which time and history have dulled our sensibilities and inured us to the negative aspects of popular theatre that seemed so important to middle-class critics in the nineteenth century. For while the terminology and tone of Charles Seccombe's sermon may seem clearly outdated, his concerns revolve around issues of enduring relevance.

As far back as Plato's time, philosophers worried about the morally corrosive aspects of theatrical performance. To speak someone else's words and to wear someone else's clothes meant hiding one's own identity. In a world where ancestry, locality, and vocation determined social status and identity, the disguise inherent in acting out a dramatic role threatened the core values of society. Acting implied that identities could be changed, that one was not bound by bloodlines, nationality, or occupation. That idea contained the essence of egalitarian and utopian thought by challenging the legitimacy of static identities inherited from the past. But it also threatened the search for authentic self-knowledge. On stage actors deliberately falsify their identities; they speak and act inauthentically. As literary scholar Michael Bristol points out, "An actor is not just someone whose speech is 'dissembling'; the deeper problem is that he is most valued for his ability to dissemble convincingly."[2]

To nineteenth-century Americans like Reverend Seccombe, the "dissembling" of theatre presented a challenge to established order and morality. These critics feared that nothing "genuine" or "refined" could come from a sphere of activity devoted to false representations and masked identities. Furthermore, they recognized that theatre "time" presented an alternative to work time, pitting the pleasures of leisure against the responsibilities of labor. Theatre attendance enabled individuals to play out fictive scenarios of changed identities, to escape from the surveillance and supervision of moral authorities and institutions. The fantasy world of the theatrical stage encouraged audiences to pursue personal desires and passions at the expense of their socially prescribed responsibilities.

Yet audiences embraced the new possibilites presented by commercial theatre with enthusiasm. Unlike the wedding celebration or community festival, the theatre assembled an audience with no shared history, with no reciprocal responsibilities and obligations. Theatergoers in nineteenth-century America shared intimate and personal cultural moments with strangers. Yet the unfamiliarity of the crowd provided a kind of protective cover—a "privacy in public" whereby

7. Interior of the Grand Opera House, St. Paul. The Grand opened on April 2, 1883 and was owned, along with the Bijou Opera House in Minneapolis, by theatre entrepreneur Jacob Litt of Chicago. (Photo: Courtesy of the Minnesota Historical Society)

personal feelings and emotions could be vented without explanation or apology.[3] Using the borrowed legitimacy of theatre's status as a form of cultural refinement, audiences flocked to melodramas, vaudeville and variety shows, and later to motion pictures for decidedly unrefined productions and performances. In the theatre they encountered a world momentarily liberated from the sexual and emotional repressions of the nineteenth century. Theatrical performances provided an outlet for expression of the natural needs and desires for pleasure and happiness long suppressed by the rigid restraints of Victorian America.

Because sexual repression played such a central role in defining the ideal character structure of the nineteenth century, sexuality in the theatre preoccupied artists, audiences, and critics alike. Defenders of liberal sexual representation accused critics of having old-fashioned and outdated standards, while the critics blasted the suggestiveness of stage productions as proof of the base intentions and effects of popular theatre. In 1867, the producers of *The Black Crook* advertised their offering as St. Paul's first "leg" show although they had trouble recruiting twenty-five young women for the play's final scene—the "march of the Amazons."[4] The editors of the *Minneapolis Tribune* railed against the corrupting influences of the Parisian cancan in 1875, urging authorities to prevent the dance from being performed in the city. The mayor sent his chief of police to report on the cancan performance and, after getting his report, forced the theatre's management to cancel the cancan and substitute a play "in which the girls are not permitted to make any improper exhibition of themselves."[5]

In 1880, a letter to the *Saturday Evening Spectator* claimed that Minneapolis's Theatre Comique, a popular variety hall, actually served as a front for prostitution. The letter writer argued that the theater easily accommodated illegal activities because variety theaters "inflame the passions and intensify the vices of those inclined to be lewd and vicious."[6] In a similar vein, a reviewer for the *Spectator* condemned an 1882 performance of Richard Sheridan's *The School for Scandal* because its "plots and counterplots all relate to the relations between the sexes."[7] The *Minneapolis Journal* complained about the Jumbo Theatre in 1890, stating that "it is not just liquor alone that is sold there; the hopes and happiness for the here and hereafter of many young lives are bartered away there daily."[8] Even the state legislature turned its attention to sexual suggestivenesss on stage in 1891 when representatives debated a proposal to outlaw the "indecent" tights worn by women in theater productions.[9]

This enduring concern about the theatre's relationship to sexual morality in the Twin Cities underscores the threat posed to dominant values by the nineteenth-century stage presentation. But the very continuity of the controversy also suggests that audiences welcomed and endorsed the images and themes that outraged many critics. The sexual repressions of the Victorian era created powerful anxieties and tensions that could not be confronted directly by "respectable" citizens. But theatre productions offered audiences an opportunity to view the forbidden and to contemplate the unthinkable. This "freedom" came less in the form of true sexual emancipation, however, than through a redirection of frustrations. The unfilled desires and unconsummated lusts of theatre audiences made them good customers for sexually suggestive images, no matter how coded, coy, or indirect. The theatre offered immediate but transitory gratification. It turned natural sexual impulses and desires into symbolic commodities to be purchased from others. One bought a theatre ticket in order to see a performance that depicted happiness and pleasures missing from one's own life. Pleasure itself could not be purchased as a commodity—at least not legally—but the image of pleasure represented in the theatre could be had for a small price.

The theatre encompassed a kind of free space for the imagination—an arena free from old restraints and repressions, a place where desire did not have to be justified or explained. But by establishing commodity purchases as symbolic answers to real problems, the theatre also helped lay the groundwork for the consumer-commodity culture of our own day wherein advertisers and entrepreneurs offer products that promise to bring pleasure and fulfillment. The

The advance sale for the Kiralfy "Around the World in Eighty Days" opened yesterday at the Grand Opera. Over 150 people will be employed in the production. Apropos of the elephant "Parnell" a good story is told. The Kiralfys hire their elephants of Adam Forepaugh, who exacts a good figure for their rental. "The Brudders" are nothing if not economical, and it occurred to them, at the suggestion of their property man, that they could introduce a fake papier mache animal in "Around the World" on producing it at the Walnut, in Philadelphia, and let Mr. Showman Forepaugh keep his high-priced real elephant. They tried it, and to fill the large stage in the gorgeous procession they put on both the live beast and the fake. The procession moved and "the brudders" and the property maker were anxiously watching the appearance of the makeshift. So was Adam's elephant. As soon as he saw that dummy he let go his trunk and lambasted the fac simile into smithereens, whereupon the brothers Kiralfy and the property maker retired to the wings and mingled their tears together, "the legs" of the bogus elephant barely escaping with their lives. Forepaugh was in the audience and joined in the roar that demoralized the ballet and the "full strength of the company." From *Minneapolis Tribune*, 4 February 1888.

nineteenth-century theatre may have emerged in part as a rebellion against sexual repression, but its greatest long-term significance lay in shaping the psychic and material preconditions for Americans to shift from a Victorian industrial economy to a hedonistic consumer-commodity economy.

Melodramas, vaudeville and variety shows, and motion pictures taught Americans to make a break with the discipline, sobriety, thrift, and sexual repression that formed the core of Victorian culture. Appropriate to an industrializing economy, Victorian values provided necessary preconditions for economic growth during the nineteenth century. They stressed the work ethic, personal responsibility, punctuality, and willingness to defer gratification necessary for life as an industrial worker. But by the 1890s, it appeared as if Victorian culture had done its work all too well. The hardworking Americans who internalized Victorian values helped build a powerful industrial economy that produced more products than the domestic market could consume. Overproduction and underconsumption threatened the very survival of industrial capitalism in the 1880s and 1890s, as business failures led to massive unemployment and repeated financial panics. The "false promise" of the Victorian code, that sober self-management would lead to upward mobility, helped provoke general strikes and other forms of "aggressive festivity" among workers. In order to solve their many problems, business leaders had to move away from the production of capital goods like railroads and locomotives and start producing consumer goods for the domestic market. But as long as Victorian repressions inhibited desires for immediate gratification, consumers lacked the psychological makeup necessary for an economy oriented around ever-increasing purchases of commodities by individuals.

The growth of commercial theatres addressed this crisis of nineteenth-century capitalism in key ways. Theatre performances constituted a "renewable" commodity; audiences "bought" the same show over and over again. Going to the theatre helped legitimize the pursuit of pleasure and helped substitute commercial amusements for plays, skits, and songs tied to the home, church, and ethnic

neighborhood. Finally, theatrical productions functioned as a kind of shopping catalogue, showing off fashions, possessions, and styles to whet audience appetites for consumer goods. As a realm devoted to imagination and fantasy, the theatre could provide a legitimate free space—a testing ground for ideas and attitudes not yet accepted in other spheres of life. Initially addressing suppressed desires for sexuality and play, the theatre became an important vehicle for creating the consciousness required to make consumer decisions a central part of American culture. At the theatre Americans learned and embraced attitudes about desire, commodities, and consumption that have come to dominate our society in the twentieth century.

Thus we can see that the nineteenth-century critics of commercial theatre had some correct insights into the long-range consequences of performances sold as commodities. They worried about the cultivation of narcissistic and selfish desires that might undercut the work ethic and corrupt relations between individuals. They envisioned an empty titillation as the core component of a popular culture that promised more than it could deliver. They feared that theatrical performances ripped out of any context of education, ritual, or shared history would degenerate into trivial diversions encouraging a fragmented and debased consciousness. One contributor to the *Minnesota Democrat* in 1857 damned the theatre as "a waste of

8. (left) Olio curtain from the Bijou Opera House, c. 1921 (Photo: Courtesy of the Minnesota Historical Society)

9. (right) Eugene Gilboe, *Ad Drop Sketch*, c. 1929, cat. 45

Detail of fig. 8

time and money, both of which ought to be employed for better purposes." The writer went on to profess personal knowledge of young men who had become so enamored of entertainment that they had made themselves "almost entirely unfitted for business."[10] A reviewer for the *Saturday Evening Spectator* stressed the pernicious titillation of variety shows in 1879, complaining that one local production was "in fact so tame and insipid, that there was no explanation for the presence of the spectators other than that they were drawn thither by their prurient imaginations and sensual tastes. The Managers of the troupe knew that their highly colored pictures of scantily clad sylphs would excite the same public interest that the advertisements of the female baseball matches have lately called out in the east."[11]

Nineteenth-century theatre in the Twin Cities helped audiences break with the repressive traditions of Victorianism, but only through a process that simultaneously assisted their adjustment to the ascendant consumer-commodity culture. Mass marketing of theatre and film productions paved the way for the marketing of other consumer goods. Once customers in vaudeville theatres and motion picture houses demonstrated their willingness to pay money to see displays of women's bodies, their eagerness to purchase fantasies that promised an escape from the dreary routines of everyday life, and their susceptibility to costume dramas and spectacles that featured expensive clothing and jewelry, they made it clear that mass marketing of other goods and commodities could be successful. Popular entertainment became an important commodity in its own right, but it also advertised other commodities both through direct advertising on drop curtains and in playbills and through its cultivation of a consumer mentality in both the form and content of its art.

But it would be incorrect to view the role of popular theatre in the late nineteenth and early twentieth centuries as completely negative, a sinister substitution of consumer-commodity culture for Victorian values. Popular theatre undermined the parochialisms and prejudices of the Victorian world by creating a free space for experiments with new social and artistic values. By promising paradise to everyone, popular theatre legitimized the material and spiritual strivings of workers and immigrants. By placing the pursuit of pleasure in the forefront of popular consciousness, commercial theatre helped fuel discontent with the alienations and indignities of poverty and wage labor. People raised in isolated and parochial cultures learned about other worlds and other values through theatre and motion pictures. The new public spaces devoted to pleasure exemplified by theatres and amusement parks encouraged new interactions between men and women as well as across ethnic and class lines. Working-class women in the past had rarely participated in leisure activities outside the home because the lodge halls and neighborhood saloons that formed the centers of working-class culture revolved around men's activities and camaraderie. But the vaudeville theatres, and to a greater degree the motion picture houses, emerged as respectable places for both genders. Through attendance at motion pictures, working-class women liberated themselves from patriarchal restraints and experimented with new forms of female consciousness and self-identity.

Perhaps the most important transformation attendant to the rise of commercial theatres and motion pictures between 1895 and 1929 concerned the changing nature of ethnic identity. Commodified culture took on for itself artistic forms that had previously been tied to ethnic identity for most Americans. Music, plays, and performances served important functions in reinforcing kinship, religion, and ethnic associations for most nineteenth-century Americans, and they surrendered that concept of culture to commodified leisure slowly and reluctantly. Yet while ethnicity was a source of security, civility, and authority for Americans in the nineteenth century, it also cut them off from other people, hindered entry into structures of upward economic mobility, and inhibited the development of consumer-commodity culture. The triumph of commercial theatre and motion pictures was, at least in part, a triumph over the divisions and differences fostered by ethnic identities and rivalries.

Ethnicity and Theatre in the Twin Cities

In 1870, an article in the *Minneapolis Tribune* called attention to the fact that increased immigration from Europe was changing the homogeneity of the city's population and producing a multicultural metropolis. The article noted that:

> The advent of many foreign-born families into the city...has made a noticable [sic] change in the manner of doing business in retail stores. We call to mind how one house in which five different languages are spoken— English, French, German, Scandinavian (all branches, Dane, Norwegian, and Swede) and Bohemiad [sic]. It is not a little amusing to see a customer enter a dry goods house and hear the seller inquire, "Deutsch?" "Svensk?" or "Française?" and on receiving the reply to see the purchaser passed on to the proper clerk.[12]

The *Tribune*'s anecdote provides a useful metaphor for the problems posed by ethnicity for the nineteenth-century metropolis. Immigration brought a hardworking adult labor force to the Twin Cities, and it played an important role in the economic expansion of the region. But discrimination and ethnic rivalries polarized citizens into antagonistic groups, each with its own organic culture. Ethnic identifications served many positive purposes for an industrializing economy, but they inhibited the development of a mass consumer-commodity culture. As cultural critic I.C. Jarvie notes, a society based on upward mobility and achieved roles and statuses needs people who view themselves as individuals detachable from ethnic traditions and inherited identities. Ethnic-based culture validates noneconomic identities like kinship, ritual, folklore, regions, and gossip while commercial commodity-based culture validates individualism, upward mobility, and personal pleasure.[13] Just as the consumer-commodity culture had to triumph over Victorian values in order for commercial theatre to become a central force in American culture, commercial theatre had to transcend the legacy of ethnic- and community-based theatre and performance in order to create the consciousness necessary for its own success and for the success of the consumer-commodity economy.

opposite:
Detail of fig. 9

Until vaudeville houses and motion picture theaters replaced them, ethnic lodge halls remained the primary places for stage productions in the Twin Cities. When a commercial English-language theatre failed in St. Paul in the 1850s, local Germans bought its equipment and put on their own productions staffed by German-Americans who had been the theatre's employees when it staged English productions. The Germans drew upon a rich legacy of theatrical productions through the *turnverein*, a fraternal organization dedicated to physical and mental improvement in the name of German nationalism. Many of the first German-American actors in the Twin Cities came out of performances in *turnverein* productions, and they saw acting as a means of celebrating ethnicity as well as of achieving artistic accomplishment. One writer for a local German newspaper exhorted his readers to attend the German language theatre as a matter of self-respect, arguing that "the reputation of the Germans of St. Paul necessitates good attendance. How are the Germans of other cities to judge us? Is it right for people to spend money for personal pleasure only to keep their hands on their pockets when they are supposed to spend something for German art?"[14]

Like the Germans, other ethnic groups used theatre in the Twin Cities as a central focus for the activities of their fraternal organizations. Amateur theatricals enabled Czech Americans to participate in artistic expression and to reinforce ethnic identity at the same time. Antonin Jurka, an important educator in the Czech community, had been an actor in Chicago and in his native country, and he gave acting lessons to children in St. Paul as a means of keeping them in touch with the traditions of their ancestors.[15] Finnish temperance societies in Minnesota made it a point to include theatrical stages in their meeting halls, and most had their own dramatic societies performing a variety of Finnish language plays.[16]

Although ethnic theatre occupied a separate sphere of activity from commercial theatre, its ties to the lives and identities of its audiences made it an important model for the commercial theatres that subsequently developed in Minneapolis and St. Paul. In order to attract audiences, producers needed to touch

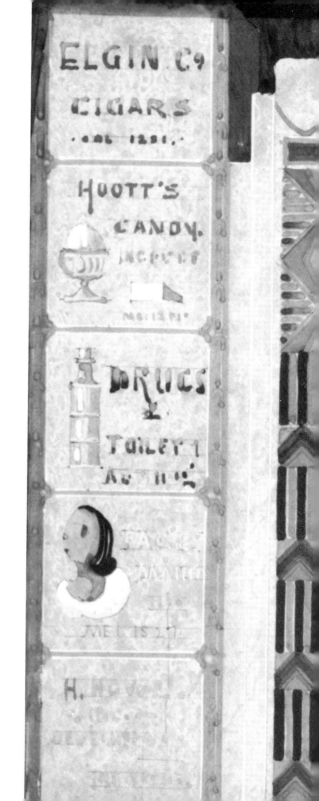

responsive chords among the populace. Just as the airing of sexual issues in a
visible if superficial way proved effective in attracting one kind of audience, the
exposure of ethnic issues and identities became an important strategy for
commercial entrepreneurs in attracting another kind of audience.

Commercial theatre and staged spectacles in the Twin Cities in the late
nineteenth century assumed an already existing ethnic consciousness on the part of
the audience. Panoramas and "magic lantern" projected illustrations (a precursor
to the projected photo slide) in Minneapolis in the 1870s regularly featured a "trip
through Ireland" accompanied by Irish songs as a sure-fire way of attracting
customers from the area's Irish-American population.[17] Owners of the Pence Opera
House in Minneapolis catered to ethnic audiences in order to establish their
institution as commercially viable as well. One of the first performances at the hall
featured the Norwegian violinist Ole Bull who was met at the train station by
"several hundred flag-waving Scandinavians" who marched with the musician to his
hotel where they made him deliver a speech.[18] The Swedish Theatre Company of
Chicago made regular trips to Minnesota where it could be assured of a receptive
(and nationalistic) audience.[19] Commercial theatrical companies learned to tailor
their performances to the tastes of local ethnic groups as well—Irish themes always
played well in St. Paul, and a St. Patrick's Day performance there of an Irish play
drew a full house every year in the 1870s and 1880s.[20]

Yet commercial amusements began gradually to supplant ethnic art and
culture. Shorter working hours allowed for more leisure time, and the freedoms of
commercial theatre began to lure larger audiences. Second-generation ethnics felt
less tied to the lodge hall or church and displayed more enthusiasm for the
commercial culture of the vaudeville variety house and motion picture theater. But
cultural entrepreneurs eased their transition by incorporating elements of ethnic
identification into their performances. Famous actors traded upon their ethnic
identities, drawing crowds as much for their ethnic origins as for their acting
abilities. The great Italian actor, Tomasso Salvini, for example, won acclaim from

critics and audiences alike for his splendid renditions of Shakespearean roles, but Italian-American theatergoers exhibited special pride in their countryman who persisted in using the Italian language, even on the American stage.[21] The German actress Fanny Janauschek followed a similar route, using her native language on stage in the early part of her career and winning a lasting following among ethnic audiences.[22] Vaudeville and variety productions used English almost exclusively, but elements of ethnic humor and caricatures of national traits played an important role on stage. Indeed, displaced ethnic anger formed the core of popular humor in the commercial theatres and motion pictures, either by incorporating the jokes ethnic groups told about themselves and others or by emphasizing ethnic identity as an object of scorn and ridicule.

10. *Ad Drop Sketch*, cat. 10

Just as the restraints and repressions of Victorian values had inhibited the development of the psychic and material resources needed for a consumer-commodity economy, ethnic identification inhibited the development of commercial theatre. As in most capitalistic enterprises, theatrical investors wanted to rationalize and routinize production—to spend their money on shows that could be "sold" to the largest number of people. As long as ethnicity dominated the theatre, it would remain the decentralized product of lodge halls and singing societies. If ethnicity could be transcended, centralized theatrical entrepreneurs could sell the same play to diverse audiences. Ethnic theatre groups shared a collective history, and their theatrical productions served to honor and perpetuate a collective consciousness. Ethnic theatre tended to be exclusive and exclusionary, speaking only to those viewers who understood its social origins. It was noncommercial, aimed more at reinforcing ethnic solidarity than at accumulating capital. In order for theatre to become a mass-marketed commodity, it had to be removed from its ritualistic and mythic functions in particular communities and made accessible to a mass audience. The middle and upper classes might be attracted to a theatre of refinement purporting to represent the highest accomplishments of the civilized world. But if working-class ethnic audiences were to give up the emotional

associations in order to reconstitute the audience's self-identification, to direct it away from class, ethnicity, and history in order to direct it toward a consciousness determined by the purchase of commodities in the consumer marketplace.

Theatre Space and Social Space

12. *Rocky Pass Drop Sketch*, cat. 22

When the Pence Opera House opened in Minneapolis on the corner of Hennepin Avenue and Second Street in 1867, its interior featured a bust of Shakespeare surrounded by eagles and angels, looking down on a drop curtain that displayed the scenic wonders of Venice. A St. Paul newspaper writer marveled at how the curtain made him "dream" despite the fact that "Venice is thousands of miles away in the old world."[25] Four years later, the opera house's management replaced the Venice drop with an advertising curtain, causing one local critic to complain that Shakespeare no longer surveyed the scenery of Venice, "but must thereafter gaze at signs which would tell him where he could buy cheap clothing, find a livery stable, or acquire a sewing machine."[26] The transition inside the Pence Opera House from Venice and Shakespeare to cheap clothing and sewing machines encapsulated the changing nature of popular theatre in the Twin Cities in the late nineteenth century. Both the "high culture" world of refinement and Victorian culture, and the "low culture" multivocal ritualized culture of ethnic communities stood in the way of the emerging consumer-commodity culture. High culture's emphasis on restraint and refinement inhibited the desire for self-gratification necessary for the consumer-commodity culture, while the noneconomic aspects of ethnic cultures and their collective histories retarded the development of the individualism and materialism requisite for consumerism. Advertisements on the Pence Opera House drop curtain provided a fitting setting for a social space in which theatre increasingly functioned as a commodity and in which audiences increasingly learned to identify themselves as consumers.

Today we see all too well the end results of that process. The nineteenth-century break with Victorian sexual repression did not usher in a healthy era of frankness about sexuality. Rather it has made sexual desire into a commodity. A

Victorian strain of titillation underscores the images of the body and the ambiguities of gender identity that have proven so effective in advertising and entertainment in today's mass media. The most intimate spheres of personal life provide the texts for an endless stream of advice emanating from entertainment and advertising, but rather than empowering individuals this invasion leaves us filled with alienation and self-doubt. The triumph of commercial entertainment over the art and culture created for ritualistic purposes in ethnic communities had important emancipatory possibilities. But more often than not, it has made us passive consumers of mass-marketed cultural artifacts that only imperfectly reflect upon lived experience. The very forms of communication that might bring us closer to other people and enable us to share in their experiences and insights, instead bombard us with messages about the world that leave us isolated and unhappy. Commercialized commodity culture raises our desires but lessens our satisfactions; it unites us across lines of class, ethnicity, and race but only in order to replace identities formed in contexts of history, work, and nationality with identities manufactured by marketing specialists and advertisers.

13. *Street Drop Sketch*, cat. 30

Yet the changes in theatre space as social space between 1895 and 1929 also created some affirmative possibilities for audiences that might yet be realized. The consumer-commodity culture did undermine the social hierarchies of the Victorian world, making it less necessary to follow orders and imitate the behaviors of the elite. The new frankness about the human body and about sexuality—no matter how gravely distorted that frankness has become—nonetheless encouraged people to seek sexual pleasures and to rebel against the sense of shame inculcated by Victorian sexual repression. The multicultural audiences for popular theatre and film productions learned to identify with and respect worlds that they did not experience directly.

14. *Street Drop Sketch*, cat. 61

In its hunger for content capable of attracting a mass audience, the commercial apparatus managed by theatre, film, advertising, and music entrepreneurs echoed and amplified the passions and perspectives of working-class groups excluded from public discourse within the "proper" culture of Victorian America. The sense of realism displayed in this exhibit and in the plays and motion pictures popular in the Twin Cities between 1895 to 1929 contained an emancipatory potential. Even though plays and films generally presented individuals as if they had no real connection to society and history, the realism of commerical genres often resonated with the tensions and contradictions of everyday life. The ascendant technologies of the industrial age that fascinated American artists like the novelist Theodore Dreiser and the architect Louis Sullivan also captured the imaginations of theatre and film directors. Like Dreiser and Sullivan, these artists saw the everyday life problems and triumphs of industrial society as fitting subjects for art, and in the process they caused audiences to ruminate on the existing order and their own place in it.

If nothing else, the crass commercialism of theatre entrepreneurs made them eager to identify and expose the tensions capable of engaging a mass audience. In so doing, they encouraged individuals to reflect upon their own circumstances, to ask themselves if they were happy, and to identify sources of happiness. The consumer mentality is not one of smug satisfaction, rather it is expressed through restless desire. The yearnings and longings for pleasure and fulfillment nurtured by consumerism can feed dissatisfaction with the status quo and bring to the surface aspirations too grandiose to be filled by the world as it is. In this context, popular culture often feeds on and exacerbates critical perspectives about society, even while it obscures the historical and social roots of individual anxieties. The make-believe world of the theatre bases part of its appeal on a contrast between the utopian impulses and desires stimulated by a consumer-commodity culture and the impoverished world created by the supremacy of that culture.

Thus the desires for happiness and fulfillment cultivated in theatrical settings between 1895 and 1929 remain unfilled today. The dreams of abundance, sexual pleasure, and communion with others have been trivialized and betrayed by the performance of a commodity society that uses our unhappiness as a necessary

15. (top) *Olio Drop Color Sketch of Cat. 23*, cat. 24

(bottom) *Olio Drop Sketch*, cat. 23

part of selling us more goods that we do not really need. But our love for theatre, for fantasy, for play, for desire itself reflects a recognition of the disparity between our internal needs and the lives we live. A writer for the *Minneapolis Journal* in 1890 recognized the operative principles behind this critique of everyday life and the lure of the theatre. In an article condemning the moral ruin fostered by the infamous Jumbo Theatre, he tried to indict the establishment's customers as morally deficient. But he had to admit that the women of "low character" that he observed there were not really evil, rather they were the victims of the unhappiness of everyday life. He described them as "young unhappy girls of the poorer and more ignorant classes, unfortunate and deserted wives, working women whose hard lives and dismal homes make the glitter, the excitement and the free lovemaking of the place a fascination and a solace."[27]

Like those women at the Jumbo Theatre in Minneapolis in 1890, we live in a world where popular culture plays an important role in keeping alive our hopes and desires. Even in tawdry and impoverished presentations, it contrasts the ways in which we would like to live with the things we have to do in this society. As long as real needs remain unmet (and consumer-commodity culture thrives on the frustrations and displacements of blocked desires), people will turn to popular culture to ease the pains and arbitrate the tensions of everyday life. As the old people used to say in the days of slavery, "You can hide the fire—but what you gonna do with the smoke?"

At the Fountian SPAIN.

The Fugitive Art

John R. Rothgeb

John R. Rothgeb was professor and scenic designer in the Department of Theatre Arts at the University of Texas at Austin. In addition to his extensive professional design credits and work as a consultant, he was an advisor to Robert L. B. Tobin on the acquisition and collection of historical and modern scene designs which are housed in the Marion Koogler McNay Art Museum, San Antonio, Texas.

The stunning exhibit this essay accompanies brings to our attention a scenic tradition which is in direct conflict with the aesthetic principles of scenic art today. It graphically represents the waning days of a theatrical style which in the last fifty years has been slandered and nearly forgotten. It is a paradox that today we know more about the scenic art of Austria in the eighteenth century than we do about American scenic artists working in American theatre in America's most dynamic and prolific period from the Civil War to World War I. In order to place these works from the Twin City Scenic Collection in their proper artistic context, it is incumbent upon us to examine the roots of this painterly tradition and the development of this style in the early history of the American theatre.

Amazingly, an examination of the earliest use of the painter in the theatre leads to the very genesis of the drama as we know it. Aristotle in *The Poetics* tells us in passing that "Sophocles raised the number of actors to three and added scene-painting."[1] At a later date Pliny the Elder gave credit for this innovation to the painter Agatharchus of Athens, and even later this attribution was confirmed by the Roman architect Pollo Vitruvius. While this information is an interesting footnote, no further mention is made of the form or nature of this earliest of painted theatrical scenery.

opposite:
16. John Z. Wood, *Drop Curtain Sketch of "At the Fountain — Spain,"* cat. 4

Of the scenery which followed Agatharchus's first use of scenic painting in theatre, little or nothing is known; however, Aristotle's writings exerted a pervasive influence upon the development of dramatic form, an impact which is felt even to the present day. If there was one salient feature of the Greek mind during this most fruitful period, it was the imperative to categorize and organize human experience as a method of understanding the world as it existed. Aristotle's views of the playwright's contribution to the theatre were as truly Greek as the geometry that circumscribed the Parthenon or the carefully balanced relation between the state and the governed in Plato's *Republic*. For the playwright, Aristotle divided dramatic form into three fundamental types: tragic, comic, and satyric. He further elaborated on these types, detailing their components and structures. Beyond these three types of plays, he recognized the 'Spectacle' as having "an emotional attraction of its own, but, of all the parts, it is the least artistic and connected least with the art of poetry" as it "depends more on the art of the stage machinist than on that of the poet."[2] Beyond this meager information, Aristotle offered no further help to the designer or painter of theatrical scenery except by implication.

Regardless of Aristotle's intentions, those who followed him passed his work down, generation to generation, applying his scant directions to the late Greek and Roman theatres. As the Roman Empire spread across the known world, the theatre structure became an important feature of the Roman city, and its design and construction were placed in the hands of official architects. One of these, Pollo Vitruvius of the first century A.D., wrote a lengthy treatise covering the work of the public architect. As a part of this manuscript, he instructed his followers as to the precise nature of theatrical scenery, based on his knowledge of Greek models:

> There are three kinds of scenes, one called the tragic, second, the comic, third, the satyric. Their decorations are different and unlike each other in scheme. Tragic scenes are delineated with columns, pediments, statues, and other objects suited to kings; comic scenes exhibit private dwellings, with balconies and views representing rows of windows, after the manner of

ordinary dwellings; satyric scenes are decorated with trees, caverns, mountains, and other rustic objects delineated in landscape style.[3]

Vitruvius's manuscript of *De Architectura* was rediscovered in the Swiss monastery of Saint Gall in 1414, and as copies were made and circulated, it became the basis of Italian Renaissance architecture, to say nothing of the period's theatrical design. Vitruvius's instructions were taken to heart, refined, and applied to Renaissance problems by theorists and architects in such works as Leon Battista Alberti's *De re aedificatoria* (Ten Books on Architecture) and Sebastiano Serlio's *Regole generali di architettura* (1545). Serlio's work had an immediate impact upon architects throughout Europe, and by the year 1600 his works had been printed in nine editions and five languages. For the theatre historian Serlio's Book II is a landmark because he included both in plan and section, as well as in woodcuts, each of the three types of scenes—comic, tragic, and satyric—as he interpreted them from Aristotle and Vitruvius. These designs must be dealt with carefully as they were the first visual expression of a classic aesthetic very different from our modern sense of theatrical space. To clarify this difference it is well to turn to Aristotle who tells us: "The poet being an imitator, like a painter or any other artist, must of necessity imitate one of three objects—things as they were or are, things as they are said or thought to be, or things as they ought to be."[4] On moral grounds Aristotle selects the depiction of man "as he ought to be" as the highest form of drama.

In a parallel way for the designer-architect, the setting then became not a "place as it is, or thought to be" but a place as it "ought to be" or an "ideal" noble place to contain the noble actions of an Oedipus or other tragic figure. While each of the three settings was composed of realistic materials, either architectural or natural, there was no attempt at a realistic depiction of place but instead an attempt to create an archetypal or generic setting to contain each of the three types of action, comic, tragic, and satyric.

Serlio's *Regole generali di architettura* met with immediate success, and the

17. (left) Detail of panorama sketch showing Father Hennepin

(center) *Panorama Sketch* (1 of 2 parts), cat. 86

(right) Detail of panorama sketch with view of Minneapolis

three settings described in this treatise seemed to be in perfect accord with the needs of Renaissance artists to systematize or categorize their perceptions of the world as the only means of understanding and communicating their vision. In a similar fashion the motif of the "ideal city" became an important subject of painters of the period, allowing artists to exhibit their knowledge of the newly discovered linear perspective. As with the painting of "the ideal city," the stage setting was a self-contained work of art related to the dramatic event but not to either the drama or any particular play. The setting could be appreciated on its own artistic merits and was certainly not expendable, as in the modern theatre. With the passing of time, strict adherence to the canon of Aristotle's *Poetics* gave way to a more complex dramatic structure in which it was no longer necessary to banish the most dramatic events of a play, such as those involving violence, to the wings offstage and have them merely related to the audience by a servant.

By 1693 Andrea Pozzo in his *De Perspectiva Pictorum et Architectorum* illustrated settings for a courtyard, arsenal or workshop, gallery, antechamber, temple, and coliseum, and nearly a hundred years later Baldassarre Orsini in *Le scene del nuovo Teatro del Verzaro di Perugia* (1785) designed and illustrated an even more elaborate set of "stock" scenes. The woods or forest setting painted for the theatre in Perugia, for example, consisted of one set of wings but three different back scenes, a characteristic development of the period. Orsini supplied designs for a royal chamber, a salon, gallery, royal hall, magnificent palace, temple, street, courtyard, dungeon, villa, piazza, and harbor. He gave sophisticated instructions for the painting of the scenes but pointed out unmistakably that, since scenes formed backgrounds for dramatic action, their coloring and decor should be generally "delicate and mild" in order not to compete with the visual impression of the actors. That each scene was a work of art, related to but not dependent upon the dramatic action, was the very heart of his aesthetic, and in this context he sought sublimity in the art of theatrical design.

Orsini's aversion to "specticale," "ostentation," or "ridiculous trivialities" placed him in the classic tradition of restraint and harmony in all parts of the drama. In Orsini we see the fully developed classic tradition of stock scenery at the exact moment in which Philip de Loutherbourg was transforming the late eighteenth-century English theatre with his romantic visions of the world. So these two theatre "architects" established the concept of the scenic artist as a painter with his training in the painterly modes; scenery became a work of art, a classic categorizing of experience to be used and reused as an art object, part of the whole artistic experience.

(This essay is as John Rothgeb left it at his death on December 3, 1986, with a final sentence added by Phyllis Rothgeb.)

was produced for theatre and popular entertainment.

Perhaps the most significant influence on fine art at the beginning of the century was the siege and conquest of Europe by Napoleon. The epic battles and monumental victories provided rich subject matter for the legion of artists that followed the emperor. The conquest of Northern Africa, particularly, opened up a new world to both artists and an aroused public that relied on visual images to understand and comprehend the epic scale of the events that were both profoundly effecting and fascinating them. The resulting art served as a visual record of Napoleon's many battles and conquests but, more importantly, through the use of lithography and other advancements in printing, rapidly brought the images to a widespread public (see Fig. 57).

Although "modern archaeology" began in 1748 with the rediscovery and unearthing of the ancient Roman city of Pompeii, it was the discovery of the Rosetta Stone during the Napoleonic conquest of Egypt in 1799 which was both the key to unlocking the riddle of hieroglyphics and, more importantly, the impetus to examine the roots of ancient civilizations. The artifacts that were uncovered in the ensuing century would produce a need to preserve the heritage of antiquity but would also make the relics available to the public and artists through national repositories such as the British Museum, Museo Archeologico Nazionale in Naples, and the Staatliche Museen zu Berlin.

The archaeological discovery of the ancient cities of Ninevah and Babylon in 1854 by Sir Henry Rawlinson further stimulated both the easel and scenic artists' interest in antiquity. What they painted captured on canvas not only the richness and detail of the architectural ruins but also the beauty of everyday utensils of lost civilizations (see Fig. 19). Perhaps the real significance of these archaeological discoveries, as reflected in the book *The Museum of Antiquity* in 1881, was that:

> The discovery of the Assyrian and Babylonian historic records running
> contemporaneously with Scripture narratives have afforded innumerable
> points of proof. From the ruins of Ninevah and the Valley of the Nile; from

the slabs and bas-reliefs of Sennacherib and the tombs, the catacombs with their 1,100 Christian inscriptions, and the monuments of Pharaoh; from the rolls of Chaldee paraphrasists and Syrian versionists; from the cell and libraries of monastic scribes and the dry and dusty labors of scholars and antiquarians, the skepticism of history has almost been silenced by the vivid reproductions of the ancient and eastern world.[2]

19. (left) This elaborate wing and drop setting representing the throne room of King Darius of Persia is from a local Scottish Rite Temple. Produced by the Sosman and Landis Studio of Chicago in 1906, it shows the influence of the illustrations from *The Museum of Antiquity*. (Photo: C. Lance Brockman)

(above) Illustration of artifacts found in the excavation of the ancient cities of Ninevah and Babylon. This was the type of visual material, accurately recording the rich details of the archaeological discoveries of the nineteenth century, that was incorporated into the scenery produced for the Scottish Rite of Freemasonry. From *The Museum of Antiquity* (Chicago: Western Publishing, 1880) 435.

This visual reaffirmation of the accuracy of the Bible's written descriptions fed an already established passion in both fine artists and scenic artists to record biblical environments, faithfully, down to the last detail, albeit surrounded by their romantic visions. This phenomenon was reinforced in the art academies and societies of France, Germany, and Great Britian which flourished during the nineteenth century. Many of the artists found that theatre, scaled to the epic proportions required to record both the political and archaeological conquests of the day, offered an incredible canvas. These fine artists developed a variety of skills that were ancillary to the traditional academic training, and many were equipped to move with facility between easel painting, decorating, fresco, sign painting, and scenic art.

As these artists immigrated to the United States, they brought with them both their passion for the epic and the influence of their European academy training. The early decades of the nineteenth century in this country and England saw the emergence of scenic art as a legitimate expression of the artistic principles that had been passed down from the Renaissance. The contributions of the Grieve family (father and two sons) in England and Pierre-Luc-Charles Cicéri in the United States ushered in an age that continued and perfected the scenic traditions and innovations developed by Philip de Loutherbourg at the Drury Lane Theatre in London from 1771 to 1781.[3]

The early scenic artists in this country were itinerant and followed the settlements of western expansion throughout the nineteenth century. As a community was established, the first act of civility was the erection of the opera house. Scenic artists provided the necessary fresco work and *trompe l'oeil* to decorate the interiors of the opera houses and, in addition, provided the stock scenery with the generic backgrounds required for both plays and civic events. These generic scenes inevitably reflected the established European tradition begun by Sebastiano Serlio who categorized and perfected theatrical settings in the latter decades of the eighteenth century.

The traditional street scene based on a European city, the conservatory, the garden, an interior setting called "the center door fancy," the prison or dungeon, the rocky pass, the olio, the palace, and the woods or forest drops made up the full complement of scenery required for all opera houses. One unusual scenic piece was the olio drop, whose origin is unknown. The term olio comes from the Spanish word *olla*, meaning wide-mouth jar or stew pot, and, true to its definition, the olio drop provided a background of various subjects or locations for a potpourri of entertainment.

The most elaborate piece painted by the scenic artist was the drop curtain which traditionally hung at the front of the stage. Compositionally, the drop curtain contained a romantic or idyllic scene that was surrounded by a painted ornate frame and swagged curtains, strong influences of the traditions of European academies. The drop curtain harmonized with the interior decoration of the opera house or theatre and, as the most spectacular scenic element, represented the

20. (left) *Olio Drop Sketch*, cat. 25

21. (above) This drop curtain was painted by Minneapolis artist Peter Clausen for the Mabel Tainter Theatre in Menomonie, Wisconsin. Built in 1899, this theatre is fully detailed in the Moorish style popular throughout the late nineteenth century. Traditionally the draperies surrounding the curtain's central composition were painted on the drop, but here the tab or "butterfly" curtains are real, forecasting the move from painted draperies to rich, grand velour ones after the turn of the century. (Photo: C. Lance Brockman)

culmination of the artist's training. An account in a Minneapolis newspaper in 1899 illustrates the importance of this piece of scenery:

> The disclosure of the new drop curtain was an event of the evening, and its advent was hailed with acclaim by the large audience present. The curtain is fresh in color, pleasing in effect and the subject is individual. The dominant key is green, displayed in the simulated curtain inclosing a picture of the "Unwelcome Worshippers." The central note is the bright red of a man's garment, offset by the tawny yellow of a tiger's skin. The insistent yellow of the picture frame is the note of harmony. There were calls for the artist, when the curtain was first discovered, but Mr. Clausen was modest and sacrificed an appearance before the footlights.[4]

The profound effect of the railroad, which connected all areas of the country together into an economic and social network, shaped theatre history of the last half of the nineteenth century. This network gave rise to the traveling shows that were eventually organized into circuits controlled by the theatre managers that made up the powerful Theatrical Syndicate based in New York. As this occurred the itinerant artists were slowly absorbed into the scenic studios which centralized construction and scene painting in the larger communities, using the railroad to move the scenery to the customer. Scenic artists were hired by these studios to paint interiors, palaces, or foliage according to their perceived talents. As the studio system became a reality, the age of the romantic traveling artist was doomed, and he became a part of a merchandizing and "factory" environment that placed emphasis on perfection of process and profit.

Studying only the scenic artists' contributions to the legitimate theatre denies a full understanding of the extensive variety of entertainment scenic artists made possible during the nineteenth century. Two of the most important were the cyclorama, which surrounded the audience with painted scenery, and the panorama, which was a large continuous canvas presented to the audience in short segments behind a portable proscenium arch or frame.

The idea of panoramas has been attributed to Robert Barker of Edinburgh,

Scotland in 1787. His first successful attempt was in a circular exhibit hall in Leicester Square, London, where he displayed the English fleet at anchor between Portsmouth and the Isle of Wight.[5] Panoramic paintings quickly spread to Germany and France, and early records indicate that the first panoramas there served either as newsreels recording the epic battles of the Napoleonic era or as travelogues featuring the scenic wonders of a great city such as Rome or London.

By 1840, panoramas had developed wide appeal in the United States, and everyone east of the Mississippi witnessed a rush of scenic newsreels and travelogues.[6] In order to make the panoramas more accessible to the public and easier to transport, the traditional method of surrounding the audience with scenery was abandoned for painting the panoramas on long continuous reels that passed behind a small portable frame. One of the favorite subjects of American panoramists was the "Father of Waters," the Mississippi River, and as many as eight panoramas of varying lengths were painted on this subject.

Perhaps the most famous of the Mississippi panoramas was painted by John Banvard of St. Louis in 1846. Billed as "The Biggest Picture in the World" or the "Three Mile Painting," his panorama took the viewer on a journey starting at the confluence of the Mississippi and Missouri rivers, moving past St. Louis and Vicksburg, and ending at the Delta of the river beyond New Orleans.[7] The panorama presentation was accompanied by a romantic lecture, usually provided by the painter himself, describing the hardships of the sketching journey and his encounters with the Indians and rustics, tales which surely delighted audiences.

Panoramas flourished during the 1850s but were gradually replaced by a larger undertaking of the scenic artist called a cyclorama. Although the early panorama was conceived as a painting that surrounded the audience, this idea was abandoned for a format that presented the complete work in small segments. The cycloramist perfected the early panoramic form using a combination of painted circular backdrops, standardized at 50 feet high by 400 feet long, and three-dimensional dioramic foregrounds executed using tons of earth, logs, live and dead trees.[8]

22. This illustration appeared in the December 16, 1848 issue of *Scientific American*. It detailed the mechanism that John Banvard used to unreel his moving panorama of the Mississippi River. A small proscenium arch framing the composition concealed the worm gears, cranks, pulleys, and reels.

The cycloramists were German immigrants mainly from Düsseldorf and Munich. They settled near Milwaukee and painted their large pictures with subject matter that focused on Civil War themes including the battles of Atlanta and Gettysburg (see Fig. 33) and on religious subjects. An account of the visual effect of the early cycloramas is found in an 1886 article entitled "How the Great Panorama is Made":

> For so skillfully is the foreground blended into the painted scene upon the canvas, that, but for the silence, the spectator seems actually to stand in the midst of a real battle.... The aim of the battle panorama is to reproduce not only the field of conflict, as it was at the time, but also the most striking

events of the battle as they would have appeared to a spectator from the same point.[9]

Cycloramas toured the country and were housed in circular buildings that were specially designed to give the spectator a protected spot from which "to view the battle or witness the day of crucifixion." An account by a local newspaper described the remains after the last showing of *The Battle of Atlanta* in Minneapolis (March 1888):

> Grinning up from between the rails [reference to the railroad tracks in the cyclorama building on which the large machinery that unfurled or rolled the large canvas cyclorama tracked] at the passer-by this morning was a head whose staring eyes were ghastly, even after a kick had shown the whole to be a mere wooden model. Near by lay an arm with the Union blue sleeve still clinging round it, and then came a foot, and so piece by piece, the curious eye discovered all of the anatomy of the same dead soldier whose unattended plight had elicited the sympathy of the woman who thought the panorama was real.[10]

One interesting use of the scenic artist's talent was in painting the backdrops that accompanied the rituals of many fraternal orders that originated in this country from 1880 to the turn of the century. The need for scenic invention for various fraternities is supported by the *Cyclopaedia of Fraternities* written in 1896:

> The probable extent of the influence of secret society life may be inferred from the fact that more than 6,000,000 Americans are members of 300 such organizations which confer about 1,000 degrees on 200,000 novitiates annually, aided, in instances, by a wealth of paraphernalia and dramatic ceremonial which rival modern stage effects.[11]

Of the various fraternal organizations, the Scottish Rite of Freemasonry made the most extensive use of scenery in its initiation. The phenomenal growth of Freemasonry and the ensuing number of Blue Lodges and Scottish Rite Temples built as a result of western expansion required a steady stream of scenery to back the religious and historical Rite. The initiation ceremonies, revealed to the candidates by various degrees, were taught by means of allegories involving legend and symbol and requiring both scenery and costumes.

The Scottish Rite originated in Paris in 1754 and first appeared in this country in Charleston, South Carolina in 1801.[12] At first, the degrees were enacted with small props, scenic pieces, and costumes. By the end of the nineteenth century, the Rite utilized all the scenic accoutrements that were found on the legitimate stage. Why the initiation became so theatrical and lavish in presentation is not known. Perhaps the discovery of the lost artifacts of ancient civilizations during the first half of the nineteenth century fed the need to document accurately the visual presentation of the Rite, or the Victorian propensity towards orientalism in art, reflecting the exploration and documentation of Egypt and the Near East, contributed to the Masonic presentation and was duplicated in the scenery.

The skills that were developed in the European academies flourished in scenic art in the United States in the nineteenth century on a grand scale. Not only was this apparent in the theatre but, perhaps, even more so in the great panoramas of the Mississippi or the Civil War, in religious cycloramas, and in the exquisite settings painted for the Scottish Rite of Freemasonry. All of these were epic in scale because the artists wanted to record their perceptions of the grandeur of nature and the struggle of man against nature or man against man with faithful accuracy. Perhaps the late nineteenth-century scenic artists had a premonition that all aspects of life were drastically changing under the crush of modernization and their recorded world would be a chronicle of that earlier life and experience. Unfortunately the fruits of their romantic visions have disappeared and were, in the end, as ephemeral as our understanding and appreciation of the scenic art that accompanied and was so important to nineteenth-century theatre.

Although scenic artists spent incredible energy to document their world, their visions still contained a romantic perspective resulting in pictures and stage settings of propriety and beauty. The camera unfortunately told the truth, and

23. (left) John Z. Wood, *Masonic Drop Sketch*, cat. 64

24. (above) *Masonic Drop Sketch*, cat. 69

twentieth-century America was more interested in the factual than the romantic dream of Edward Burne-Jones for "a land no one can define or remember, only desire...."[13]

Perhaps an evaluation of the importance of this period is best stated by the noted theatre scene designer and historian Donald Oenslager who stated that:

> With the twentieth century, painted scenery was thrown out of the theatre because it was believed too artificial by those who care more for expensive solidity than painted fragility. Yet surely it has a real place in the theatre today, if only because it is theatrical and artificial. The techniques of the old-style scene painter can open up a world of invention for today's designer if he will put its ancient tradition to use.[14]

The Scenic Backdrop—
Some Comments on the Influences of "Modernism"

Forrest A. Newlin

Forrest A. Newlin is associate professor and University theatre designer in the Department of Theatre Arts at Texas Tech University, Lubbock. He has recently returned from Taiwan where he was a visiting professor at the National Institute of the Arts on a Fulbright Lectureship appointment.

Stage decoration of the late nineteenth and early twentieth centuries came under many and varied influences from within the theatre and without. From within, the "New Stagecraft" movement called for an abandonment of the painted scenic backdrop in favor of three-dimensional scenic elements. From without, increasingly influential art movements in Europe, such as Impressionism, offered new painting styles to the scene painter. And technological innovations from the electric light to the offset printing press left their mark on the public taste and its appreciation of scenic verisimilitude. These and other innovations significantly affected the look and uses of the painted scenic backdrop as it found its place in the theatre of the twentieth century.

The scenic backdrop had its beginning over three hundred years ago in the court masques of Europe. As a visual spectacle, it was overwhelming and for its appreciation depended neither on the place it represented nor on the performance it decorated. It had a life of its own. Courtiers reveled in the scenic artists' talents for creating palaces of wonder and dreamlike visions beyond earthly existence. The creation of space where there was none—through the phenomenon of linear perspective—and the magic of myths—with flying machines and illusions of fire and water—were the stock in trade of these scenic artists.

opposite:
25. *Olio Drop Sketch*, cat. 50

Eventually, after centuries of literary dominance, the scenic artist became a mere describer of place, of locale. His focus shifted away from the visual marvels of the stage decor, away from the imaginary, to the literal presentation of a scene, and to an intellectual understanding of the dramatic action. No longer was the theatre a world of miracle and fantasy, but one of facts and earthly reason. The twentieth century, however, has witnessed a revitalization of scenic art. The musical theatre of vaudeville, the revue, and American musical comedy have all found the painted backdrop to be their best form of scenery. Not only did this age-old tradition prove practical because of its ease in scene changing, but also because of the magic it created in the theatre. The light, bright, and colorful character of nonrealistic painting styles was appropriate to the musical show, and the painted backdrops were less expensive to produce than the heavier constructed scenery of the "New Stagecraft."

Scenic artists—stage designers—of the modern period have been free to choose from a multitude of stylistic influences. Some of the major influences are readily apparent in the sketches of scenic drops in the Twin City Scenic Collection and will be discussed under the following headings: 1) technological changes, 2) Impressionism in easel painting, 3) the Ballets Russes designs of Léon Bakst, 4) the Art Deco style in decoration, and 5) the illustrator's art.

Technological Changes

In the world of the theatre, the twentieth century has been a time of technological change. As the camera helped to alter the course of painting in the nineteenth century, so the electric light encouraged changes in the theatre in the twentieth century. No longer could stage decor hide in the soft glow of gaslight; it had, rather, to face the harsh reality of the electric light's hard glare. When viewed under the electric spotlight, the beautiful illusion of the nineteenth-century backdrop suddenly lost its charm and seemed only a false attempt at reality, a false attempt to represent place. This realization, however, inspired a desire to forsake the reality of place for the "reality" of the painted backdrop. It again had a life of its own, and, as in the court masques of centuries ago, the audience could take pleasure in the scenic drop for its theatricality. Thus it followed that the painted drop might take on a style and color beyond reality; it might recall a painting style or even the work of an individual easel artist or illustrator.

Most easily transferred to the scenic artist's work and most readily identified in the work of twentieth-century stage designers in America is the influence of the late nineteenth-century French Impressionist easel painters and their experiments with color and light. Joseph Urban, a designer of the "New Stagecraft," made an important contribution to scenic design by combining his borrowings from French easel artists with the new lighting techniques in the theatre. Urban, an Austrian who immigrated to the United States in 1911, was well known for his use of a broken-color technique which he termed "pointillage." Pointillage derived from Claude Monet's studies on the effects of light on color and Georges Seurat's "pointillist" method of applying tiny dots of paint to a canvas which were then mixed chromatically into solid areas of color in the viewer's eye. Unlike Monet and Seurat, however, Urban had the advantage of controlling the quality and color of light striking his canvases.

Using his pointillage system Urban painted a single canvas with points or dabs of all of the colors that he intended to bring out in a particular scene. From a distance, the points were not visible individually but simply gave the effect of a textured surface. Color does not exist on the stage until it is called forth by a light having an element of the same color; therefore, when a red light was thrown on one of Urban's canvases, only those dabs having the ability to reflect red light became visible. The others retired into darkness, giving the surface the appearance of only one color at a time.

Urban perfected this technique of "painting" with light, and his influence as a scenic designer shaped the theatre, particularly the musical theatre, of the 1920s. He achieved fame for his broken-color designs for the Metropolitan Opera's 1917

Impressionism in Easel Painting

production of *Faust* as well as for his work for Florenz Ziegfeld, Sigmund Romberg, Jerome Kern, George Gershwin, and Richard Rogers. Urban's show curtain for the 1928 Ziegfeld production of *Showboat* was a particularly beautiful example of his pointillage technique, yet it was also reminiscent of the scenic drops used for vaudeville and variety olios and of the ad curtains so popular at the turn of the century. In this way Urban blended the old with the new, the traditions of the easel artist with the technological advancements of the modern theatre. "Joseph Urban brought to America the traditions and advanced taste of continental stagecraft. He was not essentially an innovative designer, but the American theatre was ready for and receptive to his practical reforms."[1]

26. (above) *Palace Drop Sketch*, cat. 58

27. (right) Joseph Urban designed this drop or show curtain in 1928 for the premier production of *Showboat*. (Photo: Courtesy of Joseph Urban Papers, Rare Book and Manuscript Library, Columbia University)

The modernist movement's return to the use of the painted backdrop began with Sergei Diaghilev's Ballets Russes performances of 1909 and probably more specifically with the successful production of *Schéhérazade* the following year. Léon Bakst's brilliant designs for this oriental ballet related back to the orientalism of some late Victorian scenic art, but the dazzling intensity of his pure colors reformed the gentle tonalities of that era and changed the palette of the western world.

In *Schéhérazade*, Bakst not only used rich color harmonies but juxtaposed color complements to further intensify the visual impact. Blue and green combinations like sapphires and emeralds were set next to each other in mountings of gold and silver. Perhaps influenced by his Russian heritage, Bakst brought all of the brightness of the East to the stage, and the intense colors of Persia, India, and China, derived from the blossoms of flowers and the feathers of exotic birds, mixed with liberal amounts of silver and gold, became the new color schemes for theatrical backdrops. "As a painter, Bakst knew how to release color in a stage scene to visualize the sound of music and also how to employ color symbolically in order to convey to the audience specific impressions and emotions."[2]

The color explosion that followed the 1909-10 season of the Ballets Russes is apparent in virtually every sketch for a stage drop in the exhibition. The richly textured orange velour of the portal in Figure VII, for example, contrasts with the emerald green marble pilasters with amethyst veining, all of which are set against the soft gold vista of a palace staircase, truly a riot of vibrant color.

The Art Deco style, originally known as Art Moderne, was a classical style in that it relied on a balanced, often symmetrical composition of vertical and horizontal elements. The name itself is an abbreviation of the first international exhibition of objects in the style—the Exposition Internationale des Arts Décoratifs et Industriels Modernes—held in Paris in 1925. The style had its origins before World War I and enjoyed its greatest popularity between 1910 and 1935.

The Art Deco movement grew out of the flamboyantly curvilinear, late

The Ballets Russes Designs of Léon Bakst

28. Setting for *Schéhérazade* designed by Léon Bakst for the 1909-10 season of the Ballets Russes. From *The Decorative Art of Léon Bakst* (Dover Publications, Inc.).

The Art Deco Style in Decoration

29. Eugene Gilboe, *Ad Drop Sketch*, c. 1929, cat. 44

The Illustrator's Art

30. *Olio Drop Sketch*, cat. 54

nineteenth-century style of Art Nouveau, seemingly as an attempt to find a form of expression appropriate to the new century. The fantasy of Art Nouveau lingered on, however, in the use of exotic motifs, first as a means to soften Art Deco's rectilinear, somewhat static compositions and later to distract a public faced with the hardships of economic depression. Tropical birds, palm trees, and festoons of colorful flowers were favorite decorative themes, as were those from faraway places and civilizations, particularly those of Mexico and Africa. The sensational discovery of the tomb and treasure of Tutankhamen in 1922 added Egyptian elements to the decorative vocabulary. The Aztec civilization of Mexico and the early Indian cultures of the American Southwest also furnished material for the arts.

The new Art Deco style found yet another avenue of expression when in entered the public theatre to serve as decor for the stage. Painted architectural forms took on Art Deco's symmetrical rectilinearity, and palm trees surrounded vistas of desert oases and other exotic locales. The vibrant colors and metallic gold accents which had first appeared in scenery influenced by the designs of Léon Bakst were equally appropriate in those affected by the Art Deco style.

The rapid development of printing processes at the beginning of the twentieth century put magazines into most American homes where they served as primary forms of entertainment. These magazines were filled with illustrated stories and advertisements created by illustrators who often had quite distinctive styles. These styles were just as likely to be copied on scenic backdrops as those of the more critically acclaimed fine artists, and the illustrator's art, therefore, needs to be considered as an influence on the design and painting style of the scenic artist's craft.

One of the best known and most often copied illustrators was Maxfield Parrish. His distinctive use of color and the sheer beauty of his works were unmistakable, and a number of the sketches in the Twin City Scenic Collection were clearly based on Parrish's art. Figure 30, for example, appears almost to be a copy of a Parrish scene entitled "Daybreak," only here Parrish's predominantly blue tonalities have been changed to an amber-orange palette, suggesting a sunset rather than a sunrise.

The illustrator's influence also appears in the fantasylike forest in Figure 31. Reminiscent of a colorful woodland glen in such Walt Disney films as *Bambi*, this sketch indicates that not only the illustrator but also the scenic artist added a new dimension to animated films, and often it was the same scenic artist who no longer could find work in the theatre who went to Hollywood to translate his style into another medium.

Scenic artists of this century have drawn from a wide range of stylistic influences. From French Impressionism came texture and a painting technique that could be enhanced by the electric light. The Ballets Russes brought to the stage a color intensity of heightened emotion and fantasy. The illustrator added a charm and beauty of color that not even the motion picture could resist as it turned to cartoons and then to animated films. And the musical theatre—vaudeville, variety, and the musical comedy—came forth with painted scenery of such imagination and wonder as had not been seen before. Whether voluntarily or involuntarily, the major social and artistic movements of the day influenced all stylistic developments in the theatre.

Today many artists work with projected scenic effects and stage machines that rely more on technology than they do on art. But the emphasis in this century has been steadily away from representational scenery, leaving realism to motion pictures and television. The twentieth-century stage has come to share a life once again with painting and sculpture—the plastic arts—in scenic designs that appeal to us directly through the magic and wonder that we have always found in them.

Conclusion

31. *Wood Drop Sketch*, cat. 63

Late Nineteenth-Century Popular and Theatrical Events in Minneapolis and St. Paul:
A Microcosm of Entertainment

Lawrence J. Hill

Lawrence J. Hill is associate professor and lighting designer in the Department of Theatre Arts at the University of North Dakota, Grand Forks, and recently completed researching and documenting existing North Dakota opera houses with a fellowship from the North Dakota Humanities Council.

The Twin Cities of Minneapolis and St. Paul were not unique entertainment centers in the last half of the nineteenth century, and they were off the beaten track of the major theatrical routes across the center of the United States. But their theatres and popular entertainments, nevertheless, represented a microcosm of late nineteenth-century American taste both in the diversity of their entertainment forms and in the demands of their audiences.

By the end of the 1880s both cities offered similar entertainments, both in the types of events and the numbers of buildings housing them. This parity occurred despite the fact that St. Paul opened its first opera house in 1850,[1] while the first settlement on the site of Minneapolis, St. Anthony Falls, was not even platted until 1849. The first opera house in Minneapolis, the Pence Opera House, opened in 1867, though a variety of halls housed entertainments during the 1850s and 1860s.[2] During the 1850s, there were over 450 performances a year in St. Paul theatres, while Minneapolis theatres scheduled only two weeks of dramatic activity.[3] The developing city of Minneapolis continued to lag behind its larger and older sister city for more than two decades in the availability and variety of entertainments for its citizens, but by the eighties it had caught up.

opposite:
32. John E. Westrom, *Olio Drop Sketch*, cat. 57

63

There is a danger, however, in reviewing only the "opera houses" and their calendars for evidence of entertainments. The spectrum of offerings was much more varied, yet all of them shared a common visual experience. Scenic enhancement of productions extended beyond the standard sets of wing-and-drop backgrounds maintained in each theatre. By the opening of the Twin City Scenic Studio in Minneapolis in the 1890s, painted scenery appeared at legitimate theatres featuring touring troupes and "spectacles," at common saloon theaters—often a cheapened form of vaudeville—and at dime museums, Civil War cycloramas, and moving panoramas. Shortly following the founding of Twin City Scenic, the growing twin phenomena of vaudeville and motion pictures created an even greater demand for scenery, stage decoration, and auditorium decoration across the nation. The popularity of each of these entertainment forms created chains of theatres across the country, all having their own special needs for the talents and crafts found in scenic studios.

The largest painted scenic views ever seen in Minneapolis and St. Paul were cycloramas depicting major battles of the American Civil War.[4] *The Battle of Atlanta* opened in Minneapolis on June 28, 1886 and ran through March 17, 1888,[5] while *The Battle of Gettysburg* opened in St. Paul on December 24, 1886 and ran through February 9, 1889.[6] The cycloramas were approximately 400 feet long and 50 feet high. Each was placed in a specially built display structure with glass roof panels to light the painting and its three-dimensional foreground. A variety of promotions, such as guest speakers, celebrations on special days and during state fair week, and "improvements" made by the cyclorama's originators kept attendance high. The *Minneapolis Star* reported on *The Battle of Atlanta*:

> "Since this famous picture was placed on exhibition in this city, June 28, 1886, it has been phenomenally successful from a business standpoint, over 200,000 persons having viewed it."[7]

The photograph of the Gettysburg cyclorama displayed in St. Paul shows the

opposite:
33. This photo card depicts "The Charge of the 'First Minnesota' " from *The Battle of Gettysburg* panorama on view in St. Paul during the late 1880s. Running concurrently in Minneapolis was the panorama *The Battle of Atlanta*. (Photo: Courtesy of the Minnesota Historical Society; Ingersoll, photographer)

(inset) Exterior of the panorama building in Minneapolis. (Photo: Courtesy of the Minneapolis History Collection of the Minneapolis Public Library)

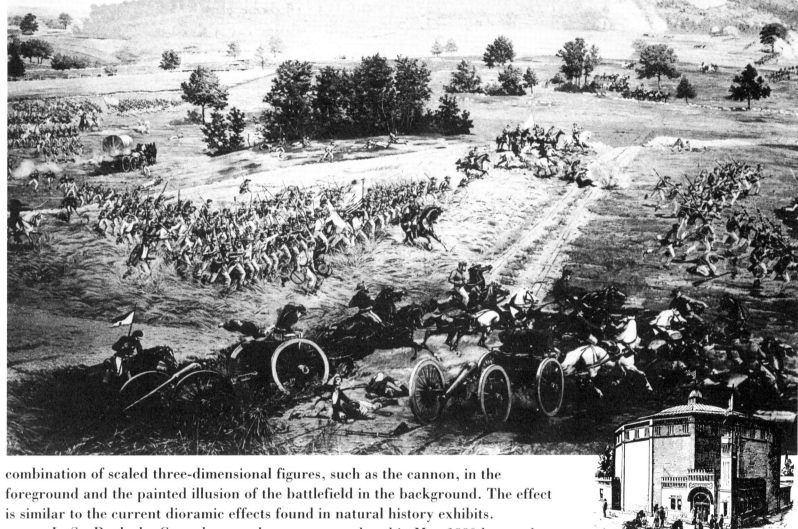

combination of scaled three-dimensional figures, such as the cannon, in the foreground and the painted illusion of the battlefield in the background. The effect is similar to the current dioramic effects found in natural history exhibits.

In St. Paul, the *Gettysburg* cyclorama was replaced in May 1889 by another Civil War theme, *The Battle of the Merrimac and Monitor*. In Minneapolis the same year, one of three copies of the cyclorama *Jerusalem on the Day of the Crucifixion* went on view.[8] Promotional materials provided an extensive description of this cyclorama and suggested, in part, the detail found in the painting:

> The people, their costumes, the accessories in multiplicity of detail, even to
> the pottery, the draperies, the arms and cooking utensils are distinctly
> oriental, furnishing an interesting and instructive fund of information

touching the customs and the life of the Scriptural age.... The shadowy, cavernous gateways of the city are guarded by Roman soldiery; through them are moving the populace. In the vicinity of Jerusalem the bright attire of figures in gala dress makes striking color contrast to the yellow sands, the lichen-grown rocks, the intense green foliage of palm and olive groves, and the gray walls of the city.... The eye follows the thickly peopled path as it leads to the base of Mount Calvary. There, on the bleak and rocky eminence, Golgotha, as it stands in silhouette against a shrouded sky, the misty hilltops all about, is enacted the divine tragedy of earth about which cluster the holiest memories of nineteen centuries.[9]

Not all of these large scenic works came from outside the region. The Northern Pacific railroad commissioned Peter Clausen, a prolific Minneapolis artist, to paint the scenic marvels of the West along its rail line from Minnehaha Falls in Minneapolis to Mount Tacoma in Washington. The artist captured the wonders of Yellowstone National Park on a rolling panorama advertised as 6,000 feet long (in reality closer to 300 feet long and 8 feet high). Designed to play in theatres, this panorama was first shown on June 9, 1887, at the Grand Opera House, just one of several exhibitions in Minneapolis.

This panorama will be shown for one night only at the Grand Opera with the best scenic appliances, showing moonlight, sunset and other light effects, sparkling waterfalls and geysers, etc.[10]

The panorama relied specifically on the lighting from front and rear to create the effects described above. Clausen was familiar with the use of these effects of the stage, as he created scenery and decorated the interiors of theatres in the Twin Cities and across the Northern Plains.[11] The review of the display of thirty views of the park concluded:

The giant geyser, the Falls of the Yellowstone, in descent in a single sheet of water of 350 feet; Yellowstone lake with a storm rising over it, an exquisite sunset scene, and a still more beautiful moonlight view were also shown. The audience was very warm in its applause....[12]

Each theatre of the period, regardless of what type of entertainment it presented, maintained a set of "stock" scenery. The tradition was to use repeatedly the same set of stock renditions of woods, palace interiors, and so on, no matter what production was being performed. An increasing number of touring companies in the 1870s no longer relied solely on the existing stock scenery found in each theatre. At this time, a series of performances called "spectacles" that relied on special effects and costuming as a major focus of the evening's entertainment began to tour across the country.[13] Each performance was often simply a group of variety acts loosely tied together by a contrived plot. Typical of these entertainments was the American classic, *The Black Crook*. The second *Black Crook* troupe to visit St. Paul and Minneapolis, the Bidwell & McDonough Company, played in 1872. Early reviews in Minneapolis referred to the difficulties of transporting the elaborate scenery needed to create this spectacle:

> While the limited dimensions of the stage do not, of course, admit of the full presentation, therefore unprecedented spectacular effects which have contributed so much to the great success of this play in the larger cities, we feel bound to say that all the appliances of the stage were made use of to their fullest extent. The stock scenery of the Academy, supplemented as it is by the several special scenic pictures and effects which, being essential to the success of the plot, are carried with them by the management, is simply sufficient to placing the drama before the public in a style of gorgeous splendor which has ever yet been matched in the Northwest.[14]

> The second production of this spectacle was witnessed by another immense audience last night.... The performance was very much improved as the company had become more accustomed to operating their machinery on the Academy stage.

> The grand transformation scene at the close of the piece had several new attractions last evening, and was the most beautiful spectacle ever presented in this city.[15]

34. *Wood Model* (2 parts), cat. 33. The two drops at the top and center of this photograph were combined to produce the effect shown at the bottom.

35. Plays such as *Fantasma, The Spider and the Fly, Humpty Dumpty,* and *The Black Crook* were typical of the spectacle dramas and pantomimes popular in the late nineteenth century. Most of these productions had little plot but relied on spectacular scenic effects to capture the audience's imagination. From *The Journal* (Minneapolis), 11 March 1893.

The Black Crook was not the only entertainment of this ilk to pass through Minneapolis and St. Paul. Others that made repeated appearances were Tony Denier's *Humpty Dumpty, Fantasma, The Spider and the Fly,* and *Around the World in Eighty Days.* Traveling burlesques of popular stage works also carried their own scenery, as evidenced by the review in the *Minneapolis Journal* about the production of "Monte Crisco, Jr." starring Corrine: "There are, of course, beautiful stage settings and gorgeous costumes. Among the novel specimens of stage architecture is a grand transformation scene; the Chateau D'If and Cave of Jewels."[16]

Fantasma, a particular favorite among the spectacles of the late 1880s, made three appearances in each of the Twin Cities. In its 1889 appearance, the promotions and advertisements claimed the production contained "15 Gorgeous Transformations, 10 Beautiful Tableaux, 50 People in the Cast, and 2 Car Loads of Scenery."

> The mythological story that runs through "Fantasma" is pleasing to all lovers of folk lore, and the scenical and mechanical effects appeal to the poetical sense. The sub-marine scenery, the statuary, pictures, and the cyclone still remain in the spectacle, but this year a new transformation entitled "The Magic Fountain," will be presented. With the backing of a silver grotto, an immense fountain is placed in the center, upon which revolve charmingly draped figurantes.[17]

In 1892, Hanlon Brothers' *Superba* toured the area with "three carloads of Gorgeous scenic Effects, Wonderful Transformations, and Astonishing Mechanical Tricks...."[18] These elaborate productions, however, were slowly replaced toward the end of the 1890s by the introduction of two entertainment forms more closely associated with the twentieth century, the motion picture and vaudeville.

In addition to the "spectacles," several other entertainments loosely tied to the theatre enjoyed quite a large following in Minneapolis and St. Paul beginning in the 1870s. Variety troupes presenting material that pleased more refined audiences toured to the larger legitimate theatres, while the variety halls and/or saloon theaters common in both cities catered to working men from the lumber and flour mills and served alcoholic beverages. These theaters relied on a combination of singers, dancers, comedians, burlesque sketches, and speciality acts—such as dwarf tumblers—who directed their talents toward entertaining an often unruly crowd. Two early "lower-class type" halls in St. Paul were the Theatre Comique, 1878, and Conley's Variety Theatre, 1879.[19] *The Pioneer Press* reported:

> The Theatre Comique, under the new management, attracted a large crowd of loafers and street bummers last evening. The entertainment was much better than those given heretofore, although there was but a slight elimination of the low, degrading and immoral part of the performance. At its best it is an unmitigated nuisance and should be abated as soon as practicable.[20]

Conley's efforts in several locations, however, were characterized as "first class variety" and continued into the late 1880s.

> Mr. Conley, the proprietor, with characteristic liberality and enterprise, has made the house first class in all its appointments, and it is now a cozy and neat bijou theater. An entirely new company from the best variety theaters of the East has been engaged, embracing many popular specialty stars, and well-known and favorite performers, and succession of novelties will be produced during the season. The refreshments served will be of the best, and the place will be kept quiet and orderly, as it always has been under Mr. Conley's watchful and efficient management.[21]

The last line above may hint at a more turbulent record of "variety" in Minneapolis where its history is clouded by the temperance issue. Any theater established in Minneapolis, such as that run by Conley in St. Paul, was treated as a new "low dive." The major saga of variety entertainment and the liquor issue centers primarily on one Minneapolis variety theater, also known as the Theatre Comique. This entertainment center opened in 1879 and closed in 1896.[22] The

36. *Olio Drop Sketch*, cat. 56

Theatre Comique opened with seating for 180, but by 1885 had expanded its auditorium and balcony seating to 1,000 plus the private boxes. While many disdainful articles appeared about the quality of the performances, the influence of liquor, and the corruption of the morality of the city's young men and women, unfortunately only a few referred to the building or its outfitting. In 1888, a city-wide promotion of Minneapolis's theatres described the Theatre Comique in its kindest press ever:

> During the winter of 1883-84, the initial performance took place in the new addition, with a seating of 800, under the present management. The improvements being made in eight weeks without the lapse of a single performance. The scenic effects were painted by Prof. Peter Clausen, of the Grand Opera House of this city . . . .
>
> [After discussing further improvements to the stage and auditorium in 1885, the article continues.] "The New Theater Comique" was formally opened by the "Silbon's Yellow Dwarf Combination," to a large and appreciative audience, and since which time the theater has continued to do a prosperous business, and ranks with any first-class vaudeville theater in the country.
>
> It is now playing all the leading vaudeville stars and combinations in the country and is open the year round, winter and summer, and is the first theater in the Northwest to introduce the popular price of 10 cents admission to all parts of the house at matinees, which takes place upon Thursdays and Saturdays.[23]

The article includes the familiar name of Peter Clausen, who later painted a panorama of Yellowstone National Park for the Northern Pacific railroad, as the scene painter for the sets of wings and drops found at the Theatre Comique.

There was much less controversy surrounding another form of popular entertainment, the dime museum, which specifically catered to families. There were sporadic attempts to open "museums" in both Minneapolis and St. Paul beginning in the 1860s; however, it was not until the 1880s that the national chain of Sackett and Wiggins established a presence in each city. The St. Paul museum was described at its October 1885 opening:

> The museum is on three floors. At the top is the menagerie, in which will be exhibited numerous rare animals, among which are a lion slayer, a nursing baby monkey, two managaboo monkeys (the first ever in the country), carpet snakes, a boa constrictor, rock serpents from Gibraltar, an array of Australian birds and other beasts, birds and reptiles. In the curiosities, among other things, are a Chinese dwarf, the lack of whose stature is compensated for by the extreme length of his head and comprehensiveness of his knowledge. He will sing Chinese songs at every performance. Then there's Little Tot, a Circassian beauty, Richard James a fat man, a colorless woman, and numerous other extraordinary things. The auditorium is a marvel of neatness and compactness, there being 600 opera chairs. The inaugural entertainments promise excellently. There will be Charles and Clara DeBaugh in a double specialty act, James Richmond and Lotta Clenroy, Irish comedians, Charles Caroles, who will personate [sic] a Yankee farmer, Gus and Willie Peters in German songs, the Ventunis, English clowns and the Spanish students; and if any body thinks that show isn't worth 10 cents they may stay away.[24]

This two-tiered theater on East Seventh Street remained the principal dime museum in St. Paul for an undetermined time, though its ties to any regional network of museums ended in 1890.[25]

In Minneapolis, the descriptions of the September 1885 Sackett and Wiggins's dime museum opening claimed seating capacity of 300 for each of the upper and lower theaters.[26] This clearly did not meet the demands of the Minneapolis audience. Kohl and Middleton, new owners of both the St. Paul and Minneapolis museums, built a new building in Minneapolis in 1889 with a second floor theater seating 500 and a ground floor theater seating 600. A reproduction of the Statue of Liberty graced the area over the entry, and steam heat and incandescent lighting were just a few of the new building's attractions.[27] Both theaters "will have beautiful curtains and a full stock of scenery painted by Arthur R. Hurtt, the well known artist."[28] The Minneapolis dime museum stayed open under local ownership until at least 1905. It was clearly a favorite in the city for its inexpensive entertainment and was never challenged in the press. During the last fifteen years of the century, the acts appearing on the two stages worked up to ten performances a day.[29]

As noted earlier, the variety of popular entertainments in Minneapolis and St. Paul extended beyond the "opera houses" and legitimate theatres in each city. In the 1890s, though, there was also a division in the types of offerings by the legitimate theatres. Generally each city had locations for first-class legitimate theatre, popular priced theatre, and then the lower forms such as variety and saloon theaters. These divisions allowed theatre managers to link the two cities as a "draw" for touring companies and created a better market to attract troupes on the road. All too often one senses an attitude in each city about overcoming the image of being a "graveyard."[30] The efforts of such men as L.N. Scott, Theodore Hays, and Jacob Litt, however, slowly overcame that problem.

The histories of the first-class Metropolitan Theatres in both cities best describe the attempts to combine the two cities' theatrical marketing power and to react to the growing impact of a national system for booking productions and performers. The St. Paul Metropolitan Theatre, opened in 1890, was managed by L.N. Scott; the Minneapolis Metropolitan Theatre was built in 1895, managed by Theodore Hays of the Bijou at first, and then by L.N. Scott. Jacob Litt held the controlling interest in both Metropolitan Theatres and in the Lyceum in Minneapolis.[31] Scott's connection to Klaw and Erlanger, powers in the entertainment industry, augmented the marketing of a combined booking for the two theatres, and Scott claimed a significant role in developing the booking system that eventually controlled the scheduling of performers and troupes nationwide, beginning with his work in St. Paul theatres thirty years before he took control of the Metropolitan Theatres:

37. Art work used in advertisements for the Grand and Bijou Opera Houses. (Photo: Courtesy of the Theodore L. Hays Papers, Minnesota Historical Society)

We had nothing like the present booking system. While I was at the upstairs Wabasha Street Theatre [an 1867 St. Paul opera house] I made one trip to New York to secure shows, in company with J.F. Conklin, then a Minneapolis theatrical manager. We would gather about 10 a.m. in front of the Morton house on Union Square and managers, actors and agents would meet all day and mostly all night.... We booked with the managers and arranged the attractions for the season in this haphazard fashion.

In 1883 a theatrical agent named H.S. Taylor made the first start toward our modern system of booking. I was standing in front of the Morton house...when he came up and greeted me with, "Hello Lou." He then proposed a scheme whereby he would represent theaters in cities away from New York and take charge of the bookings for them. It sounded good to me.

I took a $100 bill out of my pocket and gave it to Taylor and was the first manager in the country to contribute to the booking system.[32]

An event even more important to the development of circuits took place while Scott was managing the St. Paul New Market Theatre in the late 1880s. Two advance agents met in his office in St. Paul:

At that time both Erlanger and Klaw were theatrical advance agents. Erlanger was ahead of Joseph Jefferson and Klaw was representing Fanny Davenport. They met in my office by appointment.

I shall never forget that morning. Erlanger was a small man, Klaw somewhat taller. They sat over in a corner and talked for hours.... Finally, about noon, Erlanger came over to the desk and just his head could be seen over it.

"What do you think Scott?" he said. "We have got about $1,500 and we've decided to buy out Taylor's booking agency...." That was the beginning of the Klaw and Erlanger booking system that afterward developed into the so-called Syndicate when they went into the field actively as theatrical managers.[33]

38. The Kohn and Middleton Palace Museum in Minneapolis. This was one of the first dime museums in the Twin Cities with facilities for both live entertainment in the form of variety/vaudeville and a penny arcade. (Photo: Courtesy of the Minnesota Historical Society; Rugg, photographer)

L.N. Scott's many years of managing theatres and working with Klaw and Erlanger gave him the connections needed to use his control of the two Metropolitan Theatres for economic clout to attract troupes to the Twin Cities.

Theodore Hays managed the popular price theatre in each city at the turn of the century, the Bijou in Minneapolis and the Grand Opera House in St. Paul. These houses alternately scheduled local stock companies and smaller companies on the road, "...as companies playing at these houses are not so adverse to one night stands coming and going at smaller towns, much of the difficulty in getting a steady run of desirable shows is eliminated."[34]

A fledgling technological device, however, contributed to one of the more significant changes in the entertainments found in theatres. In 1896, the Kohl and Middleton dime museum in Minneapolis, now under local ownership and renamed the Palace Museum, featured Thomas Edison's motion picture machine called the "Vitascope:"

> At last Minneapolis is to see the real Vitascope, that wonderful invention of the wonder-working wizard, Edison. Many machines based on Edison's idea and more or less imperfect have been seen, but the real vitascope in latest and perfected form is a marvel that has not yet been seen in this city. It is to be the strong card at the Palace Museum the coming week and beyond question it will arouse here, as it has everywhere else, the greatest enthusiasm.... The camera, the electric light and the magic lantern are all made to do duty simultaneously in the cleverest imaginable way in the vitascope and the results are little short of miraculous.[35]

While another projection device was advertised in 1896, the impact of moving pictures was not yet significant, and major theatres had only occasional billings. But by midway in the first decade of the 1900s, remodeled stores increasingly became licensed to show films.[36] This was a major change in that movie theaters were not concentrated in one central district as the legitimate and variety theatres had been, but occupied stores and even new structures throughout

Minneapolis and St. Paul, a pattern repeated throughout the United States. In a decade, there were dozens of movie locations in each city. In 1903, the Unique was the first permanent movie theater in St. Paul.

The opportunity of the new medium was not lost on two enterprising business men. Moses Finkelstein and I.H. Ruben assembled a chain of theaters starting with the Princess movie theater in St. Paul in the late teens, and by 1929, they sold out their interest in more than 150 movie houses in Minnesota, Wisconsin, the Dakotas and Montana.[37] Many of their theaters featured a combination of vaudeville acts with a picture; thus, each movie theater was equipped for both staged and filmed entertainments. The immediate impact of film, therefore, was to increase rather than decrease the demand for scenic backgrounds. Additionally, the term "movie palace" led audiences and stage suppliers alike to expect exotic motifs and elaborate interiors such as that found in a 1929 Finkelstein and Rubin St. Paul theater, the Uptown:

> In the theater the decorations have been carried out in the Italian Renaissance manner, though there is a suggestion of Turkish design in the arches which shelter the radiators. Casteliated walls of rough plaster are surmounted at several points by small balconies of the type Juliet might have leaned from, while darkly stained wooden lighting fixtures project over the side aisles and cast a mellow radiance. Behind each of the little battlements or parapets which surmount the walls are tinted lights, their color softly flooding the domed blue ceiling and producing a strikingly night-like effect.[38]

Such sumptuous decoration was carried over onto the stage by means of the drapery, the decoration of the screen in the same motif as the interior of the auditorium, and the standard scenery needed for staging the vaudeville acts.

Vaudeville, in addition to movies, became popular family entertainment at the turn of the century. Like the vitascope, vaudeville occasionally appeared in large legitimate theatres late in the nineteenth century. Several distinctions can be

39. An ad for the first use of Thomas Edison's Vitascope, or "moving pictures," in Minneapolis. From *Minneapolis Tribune*, 22 November 1896.

40. This ad for a vaudeville presentation at the Bijou Opera House demonstrates the diversity of acts required to provide a full evening's entertainment. From *Minneapolis Tribune*, 2 June 1895.

made, however, between vaudeville and the variety acts playing at the saloon theaters. In vaudeville's appeal to audiences, primary emphasis was placed on the wholesomeness of its acts in a deliberate attempt to separate vaudeville from the more risqué variety hall entertainment. Beginning in the 1870s, troupes such as Tony Pastor's had had some success with "clean" variety. Appearing in St. Paul and Minneapolis five times between 1875 and 1884,[39] Pastor's troupe played in the "opera houses" for the more refined audiences. The *St. Paul Pioneer Press* referred, in fact, to his good name in its first review of Pastor:

> There is a magic connected with the simple name of Tony Pastor which suggests spontaneously the delights of a joyous, jolly evening's entertainment, and conjures up pleasant remembrances of them, enjoyed by thousands of the citizens of this city, when visiting in the east.[40]

The *Minneapolis Tribune* complimented the quality of both the performance and the audience:

> The audience last evening was largely the representative of the intelligence and culture of the city, and to Mr. Pastor's credit be it said, he furnished his patrons an entertainment sparkling, new, varied, and entirely free of an innuendo grating harshly on the ear of refinement.[41]

This more respectable type of entertainment slowly began to develop into the form known as vaudeville, with a particular appeal and structure.[42] While the term vaudeville was first used in Minneapolis in 1871[43] and in St. Paul in 1874,[44] complete vaudeville entertainments did not appear regularly until twenty years later. Often first-class theatres used vaudeville to fill out their booking schedules and increase their audiences. The Grand Opera House and the Peoples Theatre in Minneapolis featured evenings of vaudeville in 1889,[45] and newspaper references to similar evenings in St. Paul at the Metropolitan Theatre, the Grand Opera House, and the Harris[46] heralded the arrival of regularly booked national troupes.

Before the introduction of theatres solely for vaudeville into the Twin Cities, such entertainments were used to boost the attendance at performances in the legitimate theatres in another way. L.N. Scott's theatres booked vaudeville acts to play at the intermissions of regularly scheduled dramas and musicals. The Woodward Stock Company at the Minneapolis Metropolitan Theatre in 1898 combined "High-Class Vaudeville" with their productions; they opened with David Belasco's *Men and Women*. The best reserved seats cost twenty-five cents, and the theatre declared:

> This theatre will be conducted as a first-class FAMILY RESORT, catering especially to ladies and children. The stock company will change play every Sunday matinee.[47]

This combination of straight theatre and vaudeville was not well received.

> It would be a real pleasure to say that the vaudeville specialties which were presented between the acts of the drama added to the interest of the performance, but a regard for candor compels the statement that they had precisely the opposite effect. They broke the continuity of the drama, and introduced an element that was not in keeping with the otherwise finished performance; and they also had the effect of prolonging the entertainment to a degree that made it positively tiresome.[48]

The growing appeal of vaudeville, however, forced the legitimate theatres into booking more such entertainments. A local 1899 reviewer lamented the change in audience tastes at the Minneapolis Bijou:

> Whatever the play may have been in Hamlet's time, it is no longer the thing. Vaudeville has superseded it. We may deplore it, regret that it is so and seek for some rational explanation of the development of this form of amusement, but all our efforts will be in vain to stem the tide that is carrying away some of the best traditions of the stage, and giving us in their place a lot of silly twaddle in one act pieces, twisting and contortions, buck dancing and rag-time music.[49]

41. *Drop Curtain Sketch*, cat. 1

42. This drop curtain with a seacoast center composition was made from the sketch in figure 41. The drop, produced about 1895, still exists in Milton, North Dakota.

43. Exterior of the Orpheum Theatre, St. Paul. (Photo: Courtesy of the Minnesota Historical Society)

By 1900 the New Harmonia Hall and the Dewey Theatre in Minneapolis opened as vaudeville theatres.[50] The Windsor Theatre and the Orpheum opened in St. Paul in 1906.[51] The impact of vaudeville was evident in a 1906 listing of Minneapolis theatres and their seating capacities:

Metropolitan	2,000	(Legitimate)	9 performances weekly
Bijou	2,019	(Legitimate)	10 performances weekly
Lyceum	1,796	(Legitimate)	10 performances weekly
Orpheum	2,000	(Vaudeville)	14 performances weekly
Unique	1,000	(Vaudeville)	28 performances weekly
Dewey	1,000	(Vaudeville)	14 performances weekly[52]

44. Exterior of the Orpheum Theatre, Minneapolis. (Photo: Courtesy of the Minnesota Historical Society; Hibbard & Potter, photographers)

The Metropolitan, Bijou, and Lyceum were legitimate theatres, while the Orpheum, Unique, and Dewey were exclusively vaudeville theatres. The sheer number of performances at the Orpheum, Unique, and Dewey, and the year-round operation of the Unique, indicates vaudeville's rapidly increasing popularity. The demand for vaudeville and motion pictures caused many turnovers in a theatre's entertainment offerings in Minneapolis and St. Paul into the 1920s. Smaller theatres switched from stock theatre to vaudeville to motion pictures to combinations of motion pictures and vaudeville to remain open.

The rapid expansion of both vaudeville and motion picture houses and the resulting increase in the need for scenery, drapery, interior decoration, and specialty drops gradually altered the styles of scenery painting and the general aesthetic of the finished works. Albert McLean, in his *American Vaudeville as Ritual*, suggests that vaudeville's development could be "traced to the basic need of the American people to comprehend the new wave of industrialism and urbanization in symbolic terms."[53] The style, substance, and techniques of executing scenery moved toward the garish look of cities, rather than the earlier palette of subdued earth colors.

Another force also made its impact on entertainment in Minneapolis and St. Paul, the growth of the Plains states to the west and north. In the nineteenth century, the Twin Cities often took a back seat to the busier routing circuits to the south. By 1909, however, the *Minneapolis Journal* claimed a regional vaudeville

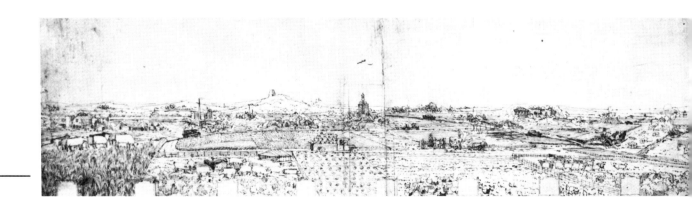

circuit based in Minneapolis had secured a year's bookings. George Webster of Valley City, North Dakota, managed a circuit of forty theatres in eight U.S. states and Canadian provinces. While clearly this circuit played smaller cities in the region, it led to an additional circuit of 150 theatres between Winnipeg and Banff. The city of Minot, North Dakota, with only a population of 1,800, supported three vaudeville houses and illustrates the growth both of the region and of the demand for entertainment.[54] Research on North Dakota theatres indicates over 425 theatres were built between 1880 and 1922. While many of these were no more than a narrow stage in a town hall, most of the communities had scenery ranging from that locally produced by amateurs to the most sophisticated drops from studios in Minneapolis, St. Paul, and Chicago.

When the Twin City Scenic Studio opened in the mid-1890s, the entertainment industry was on the edge of a major revolution. Yet the diversity of theatrical events available in Minneapolis and St. Paul at that time was a microcosm of American entertainment, and Twin Cities theatres shared with those across the country the heritage of the painted scenic background. This visual experience extended beyond the world of legitimate theatre to historical and pictorial cycloramas and panoramas, from raucus variety to refined vaudeville, and finally to movie theaters. It was the growth of the movies, however, that ultimately changed the visual experience of the nation, and the late nineteenth-century scenic interpretation of the world was lost forever to the lure of photographic realism.

45. (center) *Panorama Sketch* (1 of 2 parts), cat. 86

(below) Detail of panorama sketch with a view of Rochester

The Twin City Scenic Studio:
A Chronology 1896-1980

C. Lance Brockman

C. Lance Brockman, the guest curator of the exhibition, is associate professor and scene designer in the Department of Theatre Arts at the University of Minnesota, Minneapolis. His research documenting the techniques employed in scenic art of the past led him to discover the Twin City Scenic Collection.

The establishment and success of the Twin City Scenic Studio mirrored the expansion of audiences in the northwestern United States in the late nineteenth century and the development of that audience's need for variety in popular entertainment. The railroad, which connected all the established communities into a large transportation network, facilitated this expansion by making entertainment accessible to any and all of the opera houses in towns large and small.

Prior to this time, the scenic demands of entertainment were usually met by itinerant artists who equipped these opera houses with the stock generic scenery that provided the environments or settings for most melodramas and farces. In the latter decades of the nineteenth century, the railroad made this practice all but obsolete, and the "studio system," previously only in large East Coast cities and Chicago, began to replace itinerant artists in the rest of the country.

Located in most large cities throughout the country, these studios utilized the railroad's vast transportation network and produced scenery in an efficient, factory environment which paralleled the merchandising of other consumer goods. The demand for beautifully detailed scenery incorporating the most recent trends in artistic taste was best satisfied by the various scenic studios that flourished across

opposite:
46. The Bijou Opera House in 1897 (Sweet, photographer)

(left) Detail of the fourth floor windows of the Bijou where Twin City Scenic had its offices. All of the painting and construction of scenery occurred in the backstage area of the Opera House downstairs.

(top) Lambert Hays, Theodore's father, was an early business entrepreneur in Minneapolis and built the Peoples Theatre and the Bijou Opera House.

(right) Theodore Hays managed the Bijou and St. Paul's Grand Opera House and was president of Twin City Scenic Studios from the beginning of the company until about 1940. (Photos: Courtesy of the Minnesota Historical Society)

the country in the period 1890 to 1929. The history and success of the Twin City Scenic Studio reflects that demand as well as illustrates how changes in scenery mirrored the preferences and attitudes of American audiences.

Prior to 1896   In order to understand the formative years of the Twin City Scenic Studio, it is necessary to examine the early development of one of the most enduring theatres built in the Twin Cities—the Bijou Opera House located on Washington Avenue, one block north of Hennepin Avenue in Minneapolis. This venerable theatre provided the first location for the Studio, but, more importantly, various personnel from the Bijou became the driving force behind Twin City Scenic, moving the company to the forefront of scenic studios in this country.

The Bijou was first established as the Peoples Theatre in 1887 by local land entrepreneur Lambert Hays. In addition to his many commercial endeavors, Hays was an assistant chief of the volunteer hook-and-ladder company. Unfortunately, and ironically, the Peoples Theatre was destroyed by fire on December 28, 1890. Lambert Hays immediately made plans to rebuild the theatre which had catered "to popular fare at popular prices."

In 1891 the theatre which had the largest seating capacity (2,009) in the Northwest[1] opened as the Bijou Opera House, and Lambert Hays's young son Theodore became its general manager. The prestigious Jacob Litt theatre chain, headquartered in Chicago, leased the Bijou. Litt owned many theatres, including the Grand Opera House (also managed by Theodore Hays) and the Bijou in St. Paul, the McVickers in Chicago, and The Broadway in New York. Jacob Litt was not only nationally recognized as a theatre manager, but he also produced many of the popular melodramas of the late nineteenth century, including *In Old Kentucky* which toured to the Bijou for over eighteen consecutive years. The loosely drawn plot for this production was developed for the St. Paul Bijou Opera House and "the idea for the pickaninny band originated right in this office [Hays's] and the first darky band for *In Old Kentucky* was made up of waiters from the Nicollet Hotel."[2]

Three principal employees of the Bijou Opera House founded the Twin City Scenic Studio in approximately the same year that movies were first introduced to Minneapolis audiences in that theatre. The manager of the business was Theodore Hays. Through his theatrical and professional connections and his ties with the Catholic community, Hays recruited the business needed to promote the new studio against stiff competition from older, more established ones, such as Sosman and Landis in Chicago, Kansas City Scenic, Toomey and Volland of St. Louis, and the East Coast studios that were aligned with many of the New York booking syndicates.

Hays was an opportunist with excellent business sense. He took advantage of the growing demand for popular entertainment and early realized the potential of the latest entertainment novelty. Hays not only showed the first "moving pictures" for a Minneapolis audience but introduced motion pictures enhanced with smells and perfumes forced through the ventilation system.[3]

In addition to running various theatres in the Twin Cities and soliciting business for the Twin City Scenic Studio, Hays was president of the Northern Engineering Company which supplied "modern," up-to-date theatre equipment and installed stage lighting. Eventually, Hays was named director of the Finkelstein and Ruben empire, the predecessor of the Minnesota Amusement Company, which built a large number of legitimate theatres, vaudeville houses, and movie theaters throughout the Northwest. This variety of business enterprises provided many opportunities for the Twin City Scenic Studio in its formative years, and an understanding of Hays's business savvy is paramount to understanding the phenomonal prosperity of the Studio.

The practical operation and day-to-day running of the business were divided between William P. Davis and William Knox Brown. Davis was head of the scenic art department at the Bijou and assumed similar responsiblities in the early development of the Studio. He had previously been the chief artist at the Chicago Auditorium and was "an artist of wide reputation."[4] W. K. Brown, in charge of the

1905

47. (above) Persian costume used in the Scottish Rite of Freemasonry. From the *Scottish Rite Supplies* catalogue, C.E. Ward Company, New London, Ohio.

(right) The first logo for the Twin City Scenic Company (Photo: Courtesy of the Theodore L. Hays Papers, Minnesota Historical Society)

mechanical department for both the Bijou and the Studio, had held a similar position for the famous Hanlon Brothers, producers of many of the pretentious spectacle dramas (such as *Fantasma* and *Superba*) popular in the latter decades of the nineteenth century. These gave Mr. Brown extensive experience in perfecting the stage illusions and tricks central to this type of popular entertainment.[5]

Mr. Brown was also a 32nd degree Mason and one of the founders of the Zurrah Shrine Temple in Minneapolis. His knowledge of Masonic ritual and his extensive Masonic connections enabled the Company to compete with Sosman and Landis of Chicago and other studios in creating the vast quantity of scenery required to equip the many Scottish Rite Temples being built across the Northwest.

By 1905, Twin City Scenic Studio was incorporated and renamed the Twin City Scenic Company. Most of the Studio's business was in producing stock scenery to outfit the large number of opera houses springing up across the country. The stock or generic scenery usually included a detailed, traditional drop curtain, an advertisement drop, a conservatory drop, a garden drop, an interior setting called a "center door fancy," a rocky mountain pass drop, a palace drop, a street drop, and a woods or forest drop with accompanying wings. The demand for this type of scenery caused the triumverate of Hays, Brown, and Davis to consider abandoning the backstage spaces of the Bijou in Minneapolis and Grand Opera House in St. Paul for a larger facility.

In the spring of this year, the Company moved into a "modern" facility at 2819-21 Nicollet Avenue, then located in the country. The construction of this building cost a modest $10,000, and the space was divided physically into three areas or departments. The scenic art department required the largest space for painting the canvas drops and wood-framed set pieces. This area was equipped with fourteen movable paint frames arranged back-to-back with small paint bridges (working platforms) for the scenic artists, paintboys, rolling palettes, and other equipment. The large frame on the right of the Studio was used to paint oversized pieces and the heavy asbestos safety curtains that hung at the front of most theatre stages after the turn of the century and are still required for many present-day theatres. Both this large paint frame and its bridge moved up and down to give the artist maximum access to the canvas or linen surface.

Figure 49 shows a close-up of the bridge with several artists working on foliage pieces and flattage (wood-framed canvas panels) for an interior box setting. Artists used the palette table in the center of the room to mix various shades and colors. The palette table itself was covered in zinc to prevent rust, and it was the responsibility of the paintboys or assistants to clean and prepare it daily. The small

1906

48. (left) In Twin City Scenic's new building at 2819-21 Nicollet Avenue, Minneapolis, there was a large studio for painting scenery. The artists stood on the stationary bridges in front of the paint frames, and these open frames, to which the canvases for the drops and set pieces were attached, were then raised and lowered to give the artists easy access to all parts of the scene they were painting. (Photo: Courtesy of W.R. Brown)

(above) This image from Twin City Scenic's stationery shows the new building the company moved into in 1906 to accommodate its growing business. (Photo: Courtesy of the Theodore L. Hays Papers, Minnesota Historical Society)

boxes at the top of the palette table contained dry pigment (color) which was mixed with small amounts of water or denatured alcohol into a paste consistency that resembled easel artists' paints.

The carpentry shop adjoined the scenic art department in the new building. In this shop, Studio carpenters fabricated all of the frameworks for the set pieces or wings, milled all moldings, and manufactured the curtain and drapery tracks. They even produced the basswood rollers around which the drops were wrapped for transport by train to the opera house or client.

In addition to these two primary areas, there were a drapery department, design studios, and offices. One room in the office area contained a promotional or display space with a miniature stage and flat files or cabinets to index and store the sketches for the drops and the maquettes (profile sketches that represented the wings). In order to feature and sell the scenery, salesmen took with them a scale-model stage with miniature lines to lower and raise the sketches. The salesmen would present various combinations of the stock scenery in order to show its flexibility and to convince the customer that all permutations of locale required by his theatre's melodramas or farces could be accommodated. Once a salesman out in the territory sold a design to an opera house or traveling troupe, the sketch would be returned to the Company to be translated into full-scale drops and set pieces.

Since shipping charges were a large part of the Company's overhead, freight rates were a major concern of the Company's business manager, J. A. Van Wie, as this letter to Theodore Hays indicates:

> My contention...has been that freight rates were very excessive, especially on scenery taking three times first class, which in some of our long shipments amounts to over $10.00 per hundred [pounds]. I contend that this practically destroys competition owing to the fact that the excessive rate puts drifting artist and painters with scarcely any ability in a position to make so much less price than we can make, that it positively puts us in a place where we cannot compete with local painters or drifting artists.[6]

In the early teens, the Company was well established, and business was so good that five full-time salesmen were hired to work various geographical territories located in the Midwest and on the East Coast. The Minneapolis Studio continued to produce all of the scenery, and its local salesman concentrated on the business generated in the western part of the country. As the Company's business grew, it was no longer feasible to send out the original sketches with the salesmen. To supply the salesmen with samples, therefore, photographs were made of the original drop sketches, and these were then hand-tinted to represent the general coloration of the original design. The hand-colored photos were bound in a leather booklet with information about the Company and testimonials from "satisfied customers."

After presenting the sample book to the client, the salesman would take the order, recording the identification number on the back of the photo which corresponded to that on the original sketch in the Studio. For example, D-46 would indicate that the sketch was a drop curtain and the forty-sixth sketch of this subject produced by the Studio. The salesman would then measure the client's stage and phone or wire the order to the Company. Upon receipt of the order, a member of the scenic art department retrieved the original sketch from the display/model room while the curtain department sewed the linen or canvas to specification.

A paintboy assigned to the artist charged with the work would hang and prepare the sewn fabric on the paint frame. He would then lay out the large shapes and begin to mix the base or local color. In most instances, except for complicated

50. To provide their salesmen with samples, Twin City Scenic had to make several photographs of an original sketch. The black-and-white photographs were then hand-tinted to resemble the actual colors in the sketch. This is a salesman's sample of a traditional advertisement drop. (Photo: Courtesy of the Performing Arts Archives, University of Minnesota Libraries)

The Fountain.

51. A hand-tinted photograph of an olio drop from a salesman's sample book. The artist for the original sketch was John Z. Wood. (Photo: Courtesy of the Performing Arts Archives, University of Minnesota Libraries)

52. *Masonic Drop Sketch*, cat. 68

perspective compositions, the scenic artist could paint the details and finish the piece in one to two days. All of the cutwork and netting were done after the completed piece was removed from the paint frame. The piece was then rolled on a basswood roller and shipped out by train. A stage carpenter and artist would accompany large orders of scenery to the client's theatre. The carpenter installed and rigged the scenery while the artist touched up the drops and painted the bottom wooden battens to match them.

1920-1929   The twenties was an era of tremendous expansion for the Company. Theodore Hays remained as president, although his main contribution was the business he solicited from his many friends and theatrical associates. Even though Hays's influence was critical to the development of Twin City Scenic, it was W. K. Brown, vice president, and his son Calvin Robert, who became secretary of the business in 1921, who directed the Studio's day-to-day operations.

Of Hays's many business connections, the most beneficial to the Company was the association that he developed as business manager to the large vaudeville booking agency headed by Moses Finkelstein and Issac Ruben. The Finkelstein and Ruben circuit had links to the prestigious West Coast theatre chains headed by Alex Pantages and to the Northwestern Theatrical Association headed by John Cort. The combination of these companies gave performers a circuit that originated in Minneapolis and continued across the western United States with stops in North Dakota, Montana, Idaho, and Washington. This route followed the Northern Pacific railroad lines to Seattle and British Columbia, and from there performers went south on the Pantages circuit to San Francisco and Los Angeles. This long continuous run made the combined circuits one of the most sought-after bookings by the top vaudeville stars of the era.

The various vaudeville acts on the Finkelstein and Ruben circuit required a continual supply of specialty scenery displaying the latest looks or styles. Hays used his influence to give the Twin City Scenic Company the majority of Finkelstein and Ruben's business along with that of the Butterfield, Publix, Orpheum, and Strand circuits. This demand pushed the Studio to work at full capacity. In the mid-twenties as many as twenty-seven artists, in some instances from Europe and China, were painting around-the-clock, and still there was more business than they could handle. As a result, in 1922 the Minneapolis Studio expanded the Detroit regional office (1918-1937) into a full-fledged shop able to produce a full line of stage equipment. By the late twenties Twin City Scenic had become one of the premier studios in the country and was grossing over $3 million annually. Eventually offices were established in Syracuse, New York (1931-1937); Milwaukee, Wisconsin (1929-1932); Harrisburg and Philadelphia, Pennsylvania; and Fort Worth, Texas (1933-1934).

The crash of 1929 marked the end of an era. The headliners and stars of vaudeville, had become extremely greedy, demanding bigger and bigger salaries similar to the media sensations of today. To compensate, the theatre syndicates and chains built larger and larger theatres to increase audience revenue or "gate" in order to pay for their spiraling overhead. Motion pictures, introduced in legitimate theatres about 1895, had moved from being merely a novelty to being a formidable competitor for the American entertainment dollar. The final blow was delivered with the introduction of "talkies" in 1927. Vaudeville and all of its painted scenery was outclassed by a form of entertainment that was both cheaper and better scaled to the enormous theatres and opulent movie palaces.

53. *Masonic Drop Sketch*, cat. 71

1930-1939

The beginning of this decade ushered in a change in the type of scenery that Twin City Scenic produced. Previously, the majority of the Company's business was in traditional painted drops, but the needs of movie theaters encouraged the Studio to develop a large drapery department. Although Twin City Scenic continued to paint stock pieces for the various revivals of vaudeville and variety theatre, the orders for painted drops and wings that had been the mainstay of its business for almost four decades quickly dwindled. Fortuitously, the Company had diversified during the early twenties and had expanded its business into stage draperies, rigging, auditorium decorating, and display work for department stores. Twin City Scenic, therefore, did not suffer the quick demise of many studios that tried to continue in the scenic tradition of the past.

One noted project that the Company undertook in the thirties was the design and decoration of the acclaimed Minnesota Building for the 1933 Chicago Century of Progress Exposition. This extensive job required over a year of preparation and research. Calvin R. Brown, vice president/manager, directed and designed the

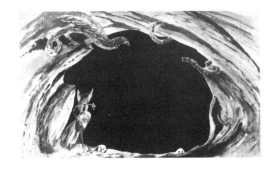

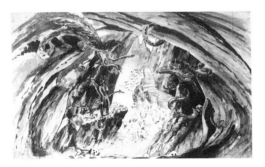

55. Masonic Model (2 parts), cat. 77. The two drops at the top and center of this photograph were combined to produce the effect shown at the bottom.

houses was evident. The circuit moguls, Finkelstein and Ruben and Northwest Publix, eventually merged into the prestigious Minnesota Amusement Company which built and redecorated a large number of Art Deco and Depression Modern theaters in the Northwest. The business relationship between Theodore Hays and Minnesota Amusement Company again proved useful for Twin City Scenic which received orders for large amounts of drapery required for the new theaters as well as for the modernization of the old combination houses called "picture-play theatres."

Clients' tastes in drapery materials were changing during this time, moving away from the heavy velours that had decorated theatres for years. A trend starting in the early twenties gave preference to the lighter weight, more shimmery, and colorful synthetics. Decorating these synthetics was a very time-consuming process and entailed appliquéing various colored fabrics on a base material of rayon triplex. The elaborate deco patterns and borders then in fashion also necessitated extensive hand-sewing.

A family on the West Coast discovered a new process which used dye/paints to obtain the appearance of the expensive appliqué. It was more efficient and gave the artist greater flexibility in creating decoration. The Company tried repeatedly to purchase this secret formula but was thwarted by the owners who wanted to retain exclusive rights to the process. C. R. Brown, however, persuaded one of the sons to work with Jack Westrom, Twin City Scenic's lead artist. For eighteen months the two collaborated in developing the proper formulas for the dyes and in applying the dyes with a sprayer through stencils onto the popular rayon satin. This process, exclusive to the Studio, resulted in drapery with elaborate, intricate dye bands and constituted approximately 50 percent of the Company's business from 1934 to 1940.

The end of this decade marked another change in the direction of the Company. The branch offices/studios became less profitable as the competition from other emerging studios began to erode Twin City Scenic's national business,

thereby forcing the Company towards a more regional focus. The Detroit studio, run by R.J. Mork, and the Syracuse office, under the leadership of Terry S. Green, began to lose money. Several schemes to revitalize these branch studios were unsuccessful, and in 1937 the Company closed both of them. Mork and Green had been early employees of the Company and had a good understanding of the scenic business as well as of their local territories. After the demise of the Twin City Scenic offices, they joined forces and opened the Mork-Green Studios with offices in Detroit and Syracuse, New York. Mork-Green Studios specialized in theatre equipment and stayed in business until 1954.

56. Eugene Gilboe, *Drop Curtain Sketch*, c. 1929, cat. 42

1940-1979   The nature of the stage equipment business changed drastically by 1940. W. R. Brown became the third generation of his family to run Twin City Scenic, and he redirected the energies of the Company towards stage draperies and home drapery installation. The scenic business had diminished to the point that the Company no longer needed a full-time artist. In 1941, Jack Westrom, who had been the last of the Company's quality, all-around artists, was attracted to Hollywood to paint backgrounds for Westerns. Ironically, the movies had virtually abolished the need for pictorial scenic artists in the theatre, and now the only remaining avenue for the practice of their craft was in Hollywood.

The Company continued for the next thirty years to serve a regional need, supplying stage rigging, drapery, and an occasional painted drop to schools and civic theatres. In 1970, W. R. Brown retired from Twin City Scenic and sold the Company to the remaining employees. Mr. Brown, however, retained ownership of the building. In 1978, W. R. Brown and an unidentified artist were called out of retirement to paint a new drop curtain for the renovation of the Brown Grand Opera House in Concordia, Kansas. Twin City Scenic had painted the original drop curtain in 1907, and, although that curtain was extant, it was so badly damaged that it could not be used as a source. It was thought that the composition of the original drop derived from a painting by Horace Vernet entitled *Napoleon at Austerlitz*. Extensive research by members of the Brown Grand Historical Committee, however, revealed that the drop was based on a painting entitled *Battle at Wagram* in the Hall of Battles in the Palace of Versailles.[8] In order to get a good photograph of the original to use as the source for the new curtain, a camera was smuggled into the gallery at Versailles. The new drop curtain was unveiled to the public on January 7, 1979 and was proclaimed "as beautiful as the original."[9] This was the last painting that the Studio produced, and a destructive fire to the building in 1980 closed the Company and ended a theatrical institution that had spanned over eighty-five years.

57. (left) The Twin City Scenic Company painted a drop curtain showing Napoleon at the battle of Wagram for the restoration of the Brown Grand Opera House in Concordia, Kansas in 1979. This curtain, the Company's last, was identical to the one it produced for the opening of the Opera House in 1907. (Photo: Courtesy of Chris Black, *Blade-Empire*, Concordia, Kansas)

(below) The interior of the restored Brown Grand Opera House.

Catalogue of the Exhibition

All works in the exhibition are from the Twin City Scenic Collection in the Performing Arts Archives of the University of Minnesota Libraries.

Unless otherwise indicated, the names of artists and the dates of works are unknown.

All dimensions are in inches; height precedes width precedes depth.

I.   Scenic Conventions of the American Stage Prior to the Turn of the Century

1. *Drop Curtain Sketch*   Fig. 41
   Watercolor on illustration board
   13⅜ x 17⁷⁄₁₆

2. John Z. Wood
   Drop Curtain Sketch
   Watercolor on paper
   12½ x 18¼
   Signed lower right: John Z. Wood

3. *Drop Curtain Sketch*   Fig. 1
   Watercolor on paper
   13 x 18

4. John Z. Wood
   Drop Curtain Sketch of "At the Fountain—Spain"   Figs. IV and 16
   Watercolor on paper
   16 x 22⁹⁄₁₆
   Signed lower right: John Z. Wood

5. John Z. Wood
   Drop Curtain Sketch of "Belangona Castle—Switzerland"   Fig. 3
   Watercolor on paper
   16¹⁄₁₆ x 23⅝
   Signed lower right: John Z. Wood

6. *Drop Curtain Sketch, c. 1923*
   Watercolor on paper
   15¹⁵⁄₁₆ x 22⅜

7. John Z. Wood
   Drop Curtain Sketch of Venice, c. 1923
   Watercolor on paper
   16¹⁵⁄₁₆ x 21¹⁵⁄₁₆
   Signed lower right: John Z. Wood

8. *Drop Curtain Sketch*
   Watercolor on illustration board
   16½ x 22¾

9. *Drop Curtain Sketch*
   Watercolor on paper
   15¹¹⁄₁₆ x 21¹¹⁄₁₆

10. *Ad Drop Sketch*   Fig. 10
    Pencil on paper
    19⁷⁄₁₆ x 24⁷⁄₁₆

11. *Ad Drop Sketch, c. 1920*
    Ink on paper
    13¹⁵⁄₁₆ x 17⅜

12. *Ad Drop Sketch*   Figs. I and 6
    Opaque color on illustration board
    15½ x 20⁵⁄₁₆

13. *Conservatory Drop Sketch*   Fig. 4
    Watercolor on paper
    16⁷⁄₁₆ x 22¹⁵⁄₁₆

14. *Conservatory Drop Sketch*
    Watercolor on paper
    16⅛ x 22¼

15. *Garden Drop Sketch*   Fig. 5
    Opaque color on illustration board
    15½ x 22½

16. John Z. Wood
    Garden Drop Sketch
    Watercolor on paper
    16 x 22¹⁵⁄₁₆
    Signed lower right: John Z. Wood

17. *Garden Drop Sketch*
    Watercolor on paper
    16 ⅛ x 22 ⁹⁄₁₆

18. *Horizon Drop Sketch*
    Watercolor on paper
    11¼ x 18

19. *Interior Setting Sketch, c. 1918*
    Watercolor on illustration board
    13¹¹⁄₁₆ x 19¹⁵⁄₁₆

20. *Interior Setting Sketch*
    Watercolor on illustration board
    13⅝ x 15¹³⁄₁₆

21. *Landscape Drop Sketch*
    Watercolor on paper
    15¼ x 22

22. *Rocky Pass Drop Sketch*   Fig. 12
    Watercolor on paper
    15⅞ x 22½

23. *Olio Drop Sketch*   Fig. 15
    Pencil on paper
    19⅜ x 26

24. *Olio Drop Color Sketch of Cat. 23*
    Fig. 15
    Watercolor on paper
    15½ x 22½

25. *Olio Drop Sketch* Fig. 20
    Watercolor on paper
    14¾ x 19⅛

26. *Olio Drop Sketch*
    Watercolor on paper
    15¹¹⁄₁₆ x 21⅞

27. John Z. Wood
    *Olio Drop Sketch of "Santa Caterina,
    Lago Maggiore"* Fig. 18
    Watercolor on paper
    15¼ x 22¹⁄₁₆
    Signed lower right: John Z. Wood

28. *Palace Drop Sketch* (2 parts)
    Watercolor on illustration board
    a) 16⅝ x 25⅞
    b) 17¹⁵⁄₁₆ x 26¹⁄₁₆

29. *Street Drop Sketch*
    Watercolor on paper
    16 x 22¹³⁄₁₆

30. *Street Drop Sketch* Fig. 13
    Watercolor on paper
    16⅛ x 22⅛

31. *Street Drop Sketch*
    Watercolor on paper
    16¼ x 23

32. Arthur Hurtt
    *Street Model with 4 Building Tormen-
    tors*
    Watercolor on illustration board
    10¹⁵⁄₁₆ x 15
    Signed verso: Arthur Hurtt

33. *Wood Model* (2 parts) Fig. 34
    Watercolor on paper
    a) 16¼ x 23⅛ (irregular)
    b) 15¾ x 23¹⁄₁₆

34. Eugene Gilboe
    Wood Drop Sketch, c. 1929
    Watercolor on illustration board
    15¹⁵⁄₁₆ x 23
    Signed verso: Eugene Gilboe

35. *Tormentor Sketches* (2 parts)
    Opaque color on illustration board
    a) 13⁷⁄₁₆ x 6¾
    b) 13⁷⁄₁₆ x 4½

36. *Tormentor Sketch*
    Watercolor on paper
    12⅛ x 7⅞

II. Motion Pictures and Their Effect on Pop-
ular Entertainment

37. *Conservatory Drop Curtain Sketch*
    (2 parts)
    Watercolor on paper
    a) 15¾ x 22⁵⁄₁₆
    b) 15¹⁵⁄₁₆ x 22⁵⁄₁₆

38. *Garden Model with Translucent Win-
    dows* (5 parts)
    Watercolor on paper and fabric
    a) 9¼ x 23 (irregular)
    b) 10¹⁵⁄₁₆ x 10¾ (irregular)
    c) 11¹⁄₁₆ x 10¹¹⁄₁₆ (irregular)
    d) 9 x 28¹⁵⁄₁₆ (irregular)
    e) 12 x 23

39. Fred J. Gibson
    Palace Sketch, c. 1910-1917
    Watercolor on paper
    15½ x 17¹⁄₁₆
    Signed lower right: Fred J. Gibson

40. *Interior Decoration of New Harnois
    Theatre*
    Watercolor on illustration board
    29¹¹⁄₁₆ x 21⅞

41. *Drop Curtain Sketch with Picture
    Screen*
    Watercolor on illustration board
    16⅛ x 23⅛

42. Eugene Gilboe
    Drop Curtain Sketch, c. 1929 Fig. 56
    Watercolor on illustration board
    15¾ x 22¹¹⁄₁₆
    Signed verso: Eugene Gilboe

43. *Tormentor Sketch*
    Opaque color on illustration board
    19⅞ x 14

III. Visual Styles in Scenery: Vaudeville and
the Move toward "Modernism"

44. Eugene Gilboe
    Ad Drop Sketch, c. 1929 Fig. 29
    Opaque color on illustration board
    15⁹⁄₁₆ x 22⅜
    Signed verso: Eugene Gilboe

45. Eugene Gilboe
    Ad Drop Sketch, c. 1929 Figs. 11 and
    9
    Opaque color on illustration board
    15⅝ x 22½
    Signed verso: Eugene Gilboe

46. *Garden Drop Sketch*
    Opaque color on illustration board
    15³⁄₁₆ x 22¹⁄₁₆

47. *Interior Drop Sketch*
    Opaque color on illustration board
    15¹⁵⁄₁₆ x 22⅞

48. *Interior Drop Sketch*
Watercolor on illustration board
13½ x 18

49. *Olio Drop Sketch*
Opaque color on illustration board
16¹/₁₆ x 22½

50. *Olio Drop Sketch*   Figs. VI and 25
Opaque color on illustration board
15⅞ x 22⅝

51. *Olio Drop Sketch*
Opaque color on illustration board
14⁹/₁₆ x 22⅜

52. *Olio Drop Sketch*
Opaque color on illustration board
13¹⁵/₁₆ x 21½

53. *Olio Drop Sketch*
Opaque color on illustration board
15⅛ x 21½

54. *Olio Drop Sketch*   Fig. 30
Opaque color on illustration board
14¹³/₁₆ x 22⅛

55. *Olio Drop Sketch*
Opaque color on illustration board
15½ x 21½

56. *Olio Drop Sketch*   Figs. III and 36
Opaque color on paper
15¹¹/₁₆ x 22½

57. John E. Westrom
Olio Drop Sketch   Fig. 32
Opaque color on illustration board
15½ x 22½
Signed verso: Westrom

58. *Palace Drop Sketch*   Figs. VII and 26
Opaque color on illustration board
14 x 21⅞

59. *Palace Drop Sketch*
Opaque color on illustration board
15⁹/₁₆ x 21⅛

60. *Mountain Drop Sketch*
Opaque color on illustration board
12³/₁₆ x 16⅛

61. *Street Drop Sketch*   Figs. VIII and 14
Opaque color on illustration board
15¹⁵/₁₆ x 22⁷/₁₆

62. *Wood Drop Sketch*
Opaque color on illustration board
15 x 22

63. *Wood Drop Sketch*   Fig. 31
Opaque color on illustration board
13½ x 20

IV. Theatrical Settings Used in the Ancient Scottish Rite of Freemasonry

64. John Z. Wood
Masonic Drop Sketch   Figs. V and 23
Watercolor on paper
15¹⁵/₁₆ x 21⅝
Signed lower right: J.Z.W.

65. *Masonic Drop Sketch*
Opaque color on illustration board
16 x 20⅞

66. *Masonic Drop Sketch*
Watercolor on illustration board
16¹/₁₆ x 21¼

67. *Masonic Drop Sketch*
Watercolor on paper
14⅝ x 23³/₁₆

68. *Masonic Drop Sketch*   Fig. 52
Opaque color on illustration board
15⁹/₁₆ x 22¹¹/₁₆

69. *Masonic Drop Sketch*   Fig. 24
Opaque color on paper
14⅝ x 22⁷/₁₆

70. *Masonic Model Sketch*
Opaque color on illustration board
16 x 20⅞

71. *Masonic Drop Sketch*   Fig. 53
Opaque color on paper
14⅝ x 22⅜

72. *Masonic Palace Sketches* (4 parts)
Watercolor on illustration board
a) 16 x 20⅞ (irregular)
b) 16 x 21 (irregular)
c) 15¹⁵/₁₆ x 21 (irregular)
d) 15¹⁵/₁₆ x 21

73. *Masonic Model* (2 parts)
Watercolor on paper
a) 14⅛ x 22⅜ (irregular)
b) 14⅝ x 22⅜

74. *Masonic Drop Sketch*
Watercolor on paper
14⅝ x 23³/₁₆

75. *Masonic Drop Sketch* (3 parts)
Watercolor on paper
a) 2⅝ x 6 (irregular)
b) 14⁷/₁₆ x 23¼ (irregular)
c) 14⁹/₁₆ x 23³/₁₆

76. *Masonic Drop Sketch*
Opaque color on paper
14⁹/₁₆ x 23⅛

77. *Masonic Model* (2 parts)   Fig.55
Watercolor on paper
a) 11¼ x 19¹/₁₆
b) 11¼ x 17⁷/₁₆

78. *Masonic Model*
    Watercolor on paper
    16 x 20⅞

79. *Masonic Drop Sketch*
    Pencil on illustration board
    14⅝ x 22

80. *Masonic Drop Sketch*
    Opaque color on illustration board
    15⅝ x 22½

**V.   Scenic Techniques in Nontheatrical
      Entertainment**

81. *Sketch of Model for Commercial Display* (3 parts)
    Opaque color on illustration board
    a) 14⅜ x 22¹⁵⁄₁₆
    b) 6⅞ x 15⅝ (irregular)
    c) 11¹⁵⁄₁₆ x 22⅛ (irregular)

82. *Sketch of Viking Story* (9 parts)
    Pencil on illustration board
    a) 11⅛ x 10⅞
    b) 10⅝ x 10½
    c) 10⅝ x 10⁹⁄₁₆
    d) 10⁹⁄₁₆ x 10⅜
    e) 11⅞ x 10¹¹⁄₁₆
    f) 10⅝ x 10½
    g) 11¹⁵⁄₁₆ x 13⅝ (irregular)
    h) 11⁵⁄₁₆ x 10⅞
    i) 11 x 11¹⁄₁₆

83. *Mountain Drop Sketch*
    Watercolor on paper
    10½ x 17

84. Eugene Gilboe
    Olio Drop Sketch, c. 1929
    Opaque color on illustration board
    15½ x 22¾
    Signed verso: Eugene Gilboe

85. Eugene Gilboe
    Olio Drop Sketch, c. 1929
    Watercolor on illustration board
    15⁷⁄₁₆ x 22¹¹⁄₁₆
    Signed verso: Eugene Gilboe

86. *Panorama Sketch* (2 parts)
    Figs. 17 and 45
    Ink on paper
    a) 11½ x 59⁹⁄₁₆
    b) 11⁷⁄₁₆ x 56⅜

87. *Mechanized Model*
    Wood structure
    77 x 56⅜ x 29¼

88. *Electrified Garden Model*
    Wood structure and opaque color on
    illustration board
    14⅜ x 24 x 15

89. *Electrified Wood Model*
    Wood structure and watercolor on
    illustration board
    13⅜ x 24 x 13⅞

Notes

Theatre Space as Social Space: The Twin City Scenic Collection

1. Donald Z. Woods, "A History of the Theatre in Minneapolis, Minnesota, from its Beginnings to 1900," Ph. D. diss. (University of Minnesota, 1950), 22-23.
2. Michael Bristol, *Carnival and Theater* (New York: Metheun, 1985), 113.
3. For a discussion of the concept of "privacy in public," see John F. Kasson, *Amusing the Million*, New York: Hill and Wang, 1978.
4. John K. Sherman, "Music and Theater in Minnesota History," in William Van O'Connor, ed., *A History of the Arts in Minnesota* (Minneapolis: University of Minnesota Press, 1958), 42.
5. Lawrence James Hill, "A History of Variety—Vaudeville in Minneapolis, Minnesota from its Beginning to 1900," Ph.D. diss. (University of Minnesota, 1979), 93.
6. Quoted in Hill, p. 144.
7. Woods, p. 268.
8. Quoted in Hill, p. 249.
9. Audley Mitchell Grossman, Jr., "The Professional Legitimate Theater in Minneapolis from 1890 to 1910," Ph.D. diss. (University of Minnesota, 1957), citing *Minneapolis Tribune*, 21 March 1891, p. 8.
10. Quoted in Woods, pp. 24-25.
11. Quoted in Hill, p. 108.
12. Quoted in Woods, p. 129.
13. I.C. Jarvie, "Explorations in the Social Career of Movies: Business and Religion," in I.S. Jarvie, ed., *Thinking About Society: Theory and Practice* (Norwell, MA: Kluwer Academic, 1986), 372.
14. Herman E. Rothfuss, "The German Theater in Minnesota," Ph.D. diss. (University of Minnesota, 1949), 232.
15. Esther Jerabek, "The Transition of a New World Bohemia," *Minnesota History* 15:1 (March 1934):40; Esther Jerabek, "Antonin Jurka, A Pioneer Czech Schoolmaster in Minnesota," *Minnesota History* 13:3 (September 1932): 273.
16. John Ilmari Holehmainen, "Finnish Temperance Societies in Minnesota," *Minnesota History* 22:4 (December 1941): 412.
17. Hill, p. 110.
18. Donald Z. Woods, "Playhouse for Pioneers: The Story of the Pence Opera House," *Minnesota History* 33:4 (Winter 1952): 171.
19. Donald Z. Woods, review of *The Swedish Theatre of Chicago 1868-1950* by Henriette C. K. Naeseth, *Minnesota History* 33:1 (1952):41.
20. Andrew F. Jensen, "Two Decades of Trouping in Minnesota, 1865-1886," *Minnesota History* 28:2 (June 1947):110-11.
21. Jensen, p. 118.
22. Ibid.
23. Jarvie, p. 371. See also Lary May, *Screening Out the Past*, Chicago: University of Chicago Press, 1980.
24. Anne-Charlotte Harvey and Richard H. Hulan, "'Teater, Visafton Och Bal': The Swedish-American Road Show In Its Heyday," *The Swedish-American Historical Quarterly* 37:3 (July 1986):135.
25. Woods, "Playhouse for Pioneers," p. 172.
26. Woods, "Playhouse for Pioneers," p. 178.
27. Quoted in Hill, p. 249.

The Fugitive Art

1. Aristotle, *Poetics, Philosophy of Art and Aesthetics: From Plato to Wittgenstein*, ed. Frank A. Tillman and Steven M. Cahn (New York: Harper, 1969), 61.
2. Aristotle, p. 64.
3. Vitruvius, *The Ten Books of Architecture*, trans. Morris Hichy Morgan (New York: Dover Publications, Inc., 1960), 150.
4. Aristotle, p. 78.

The Age of Scenic Art: The Nineteenth Century

1. Ida Procter, *Masters of British Nineteenth Century Art* (London: Dennis Dobson, 1961), 157.
2. L. W. Yaggy and T. L. Haines, *Museum of Antiquity* (Chicago: Western Publishing House, 1880), 911-12.
3. Donald Oenslager, *Stage Design* (New York: The Viking Press, 1975), 146, 158.
4. "Entertainment," *Minneapolis Tribune*, 22 August 1899, p. 6, col. 4.

5. John Francis McDermott, *Lost Panoramas of the Mississippi* (Chicago: University of Chicago Press, 1958), 2.
6. McDermott, p. 7.
7. McDermott, p. 31.
8. Theodore R. Davis, "How a Great Panorama is Made," *St. Nicolas* (Dec. 1886): 110.
9. Davis, p. 99.
10. "After the Battle," *Minneapolis Tribune*, 14 February 1888, p. 2.
11. Albert C. Stevens, "Preface" in *Cyclopaedia of Fraternities* 2nd ed. (New York: E. B. Treat & Co., 1907).
12. Albert Gallatin Mackey, *The History of Freemasonry* (New York: The Masonic History Company, 1898), 7:1805.
13. Proctor, p. 157.
14. Oenslager, p. 167.

The Scenic Backdrop— Some Comments on the Influences of "Modernism"

1. Donald Oenslager, *Stage Design* (New York: The Viking Press, 1975), 228.
2. Ibid., 197.

Late Nineteenth-Century Popular and Theatrical Events in Minneapolis and St. Paul: A Microcosm of Entertainment

1. Frank M. Whiting, "A History of the Theatre in St. Paul, Minnesota from its Beginning to 1890," Ph.D. diss. (University of Minnesota, 1941), 1.
2. Donald Z. Woods, "A History of the Theatre in Minneapolis, Minnesota, from its Beginnings to 1900," Ph.D. diss. (University of Minnesota, 1950), 81-88.
3. Woods, p. 16.
4. The author has searched archives about various cycloramas displayed in cities across the East and Midwest and has visited the collection at the Milwaukee County Historical Society. The terms cyclorama and panorama are frequently interchanged in the press of the period. I will use the term cyclorama for a stationary large exhibit and the term panorama for a moving panel of painted scenery on large rollers. A useful general citation is Robert Wernick, "Getting a glimpse of history from a grandstand seat," *Smithsonian* (August 1985):68-85. Color fold-outs of both the *Battle of Atlanta* and *Battle of Gettysburg* are included in the article. Clearly, there were two studios in Milwaukee producing cycloramas in the 1880s. The company producing the *Battle of Atlanta* is not recorded as having produced a Gettysburg cyclorama, leading me to conclude the two rival companies divided the market by each displaying a cyclorama in one of the Twin Cities. An excellent scholarly source is Richard Wickman, "An Evaluation of the Employment of Panoramic Scenery in the Nineteenth Century," Ph.D. diss., Ohio State University, 1961.
5. Lawrence J. Hill, "A History of Variety—Vaudeville in Minneapolis, Minnesota from its Beginning to 1900," Ph.D. diss. (University of Minnesota, 1979), 224-26.
6. Whiting, p. 470.
7. *Minneapolis Star*, 25 February 1886, p. 2.
8. *The Panorama Painters and Their Work* (Milwaukee: Milwaukee County Historical Center, 1969), 7. The *Smithsonian* article on cycloramas reports an existing copy of the *Jerusalem* cyclorama at the shrine of Ste. Anne de Beaupre in Quebec (see note 4).
9. *Business Guide of Minneapolis* (Minneapolis City Collection: Minneapolis Public Library, c. 1888), i.
10. *Saturday Evening Spectator*, 28 May 1887, p. 6.
11. *Minneapolis Tribune*, 10 June 1887, p. 5.
12. The author is involved with an ongoing research project for the Mid America Theatre Conference and has located references to scenery by Peter Clausen in Wahpeton, Fargo, and Grand Forks, North Dakota. Clausen's theatre work is briefly covered in the Woods dissertation. In connection with his work on the Twin City Scenic Studio, C. Lance Brockman has compiled a theatrical "biography" of Peter Clausen.
13. These events pushed the theatrical technology of the period much like the "spectacles" of the current theatre do, for example, raising the level of technology over the "book" or story of a show in such productions as *Cats*.
14. *Minneapolis Tribune*, 9 October 1872, p. 4. The company played St. Paul on

November 11-12, 1872, according to Whiting (see note 1).

15. *Minneapolis Daily Evening News*, 9 October 1872, p. 4.

16. *Minneapolis Journal*, 2 February 1889, p. 8.

17. *Minneapolis Journal*, 16 March 1889, p. 8.

18. *Minneapolis Tribune*, 24 April 1892, p. 5. These spectacles playing at the legitimate theatres during the 1890s frequently supplied drawings for the promotion pieces run in the major daily newspapers. For example, four scenes from a *Fantasma* can be found in the Minneapolis *Saturday Evening Spectator*, 11 March 1893.

19. Whiting, p. 465.

20. *St. Paul Pioneer Press*, 9 April 1878, p. 7.

21. *St. Paul Pioneer Press*, 28 August 1881, p. 7.

22. For a detailed account of this battle of the temperance forces and the saloon or variety theaters, see the Hill dissertation listed above. Details of the Jumbo, Casino, Louvre, and Columbia Theatre's efforts to stay afloat make interesting reading about societal attitudes expressed in the print of the day versus the clear popularity of these "dives."

23. *Minneapolis Tribune*, 8 January 1888, p. 8.

24. *St. Paul Globe*, 11 October 1885, p. 6.

25. *St. Paul Pioneer Press*, 2 March 1957. St. Paul Public Library Clipping on Aperature Card 11021.

26. *Minneapolis Star*, 17 September 1887, p. 1.

27. Hill, pp. 218-19.

28. *Minneapolis Tribune*, 25 August 1889, p. 5. Another reference to Arthur Hurtt by the *Tribune* concerns his work as an in-house scenic artist at Hays's Peoples Theatre, 1 January 1889, p. 14.

29. A listing of headliners is in the Hill dissertation; upwards of twelve acts a week would be listed in the ads. This would reflect changes in the "freaks," the specialty acts, and the melodrama.

30. The Whiting dissertation particularly deals with this issue.

31. Audley M. Grossman, "The Professional Legitimate Theater in Minneapolis from 1890 to 1920," Ph.D. diss. (University of Minnesota, 1957), 67. The power play among Scott, Hays, Litt, and others was quite protracted and influenced what types and how many events played in the two cities.

32. Editorial, *Minneapolis Journal*, 22 June 1924, sec. 1.

33. Editorial, *Minneapolis Journal*, 22 June 1924, sec. 1. L.N. Scott's papers and records are available to researchers at the Minnesota Historical Society in St. Paul.

34. *Minneapolis Journal*, 4 February 1906, p. 1.

35. *Minneapolis Journal*, 21 November 1896, p. 9.

36. See Grossman's dissertation for a photo of the Cyril movie house in Minneapolis, p. 191.

37. *St. Paul Pioneer Press*, 12 September 1945. St. Paul Public Library Clipping on Aperture Card 11026.

38. *St. Paul Dispatch* 10 April 1929. St. Paul Public Library Clipping on Aperture Card 11039.

39. Pastor played each June in 1875, 1880, 1882, 1883, and 1884; see Hill's dissertation, vol. 2, and Whiting's dissertation, vol. 2.

40. *St. Paul Pioneer Press*, 2 July 1875, p. 4.

41. *Minneapolis Tribune*, 30 June 1875, p. 4.

42. For an analysis of vaudeville's unique structure, see Albert F. McLean, *American Vaudeville as Ritual*, Lexington: University of Kentucky Press, 1965.

43. Whiting, p. 461.

44. Hill, p. 78.

45. Hill, pp. 219-20.

46. *St. Paul Daily News*, 16 April 1922, no page. St. Paul Public Library Clipping on Aperture Card 10769.

47. *Minneapolis Journal*, 12 November 1898, p. 2.

48. *Minneapolis Journal*, 15 November 1898, p. 4.

49. *Minneapolis Journal*, 14 March 1899, p. 4.

50. Hill, pp. 287, 294-95.

51. *St. Paul Daily News*, 16 April 1922, no page. St. Paul Public Library Clipping, Aperture Card 10769.

52. *Minneapolis Journal*, 4 February 1906, p. 16.

53. McLean, p. 24.

54. *Minneapolis Journal*, 29 August 1909, p. 4.

The Twin City Scenic Studio: A Chronology 1896—1980

Most of the information for this essay was based on personal interviews with W. R. Brown, 15 June 1983, 22 June 1983, 14 September 1984, 10 September 1986. Mr. Brown is the past president of Twin City Scenic Studio.

1. Notes from the Theodore Hays Papers, Minnesota Historical Society, St. Paul.
2. "Historic Minneapolis Theater Once More Changes Its Policy," *Minneapolis Journal*, 11 March 1917, p. 11, col. 1.
3. "Theodore Hays, Showman Dies," *Minneapolis Sunday Tribune*, 6 May 1945, p. 1.
4. Theodore Hays to E. G. Cook, 19 October 1907, Theodore Hays Papers.
5. Ibid.
6. J. A. Van Wie to Theodore Hays, 10 December 1907, Theodore Hays Papers.
7. *Report of the Minnesota Century of Progress Exposition Commission* (St. Paul, 1934), 5-6.
8. *The Brown Grand Theatre* (Concordia, Kansas: Commemorative Program, 1979), 41.

V. John Z. Wood, *Masonic Drop Sketch*, cat. 64

VI. *Olio Drop Sketch*, cat. 50

VII. *Palace Drop Sketch*, cat. 58

VIII. *Street Drop Sketch*, cat. 61